# CAMPAIGNS FROM THE GROUND UP

# Pathways of Politics

Daniel M. Shea, Series Editor

"Pathways of Politics" is a new series of books exploring key advances in the ability of average citizens to bring about meaningful change in American politics. The major routes of change included in the series are:

- Elections
- Litigation
- Legislation and Lobbying
- Grassroots Activism
- Cultural Shifts

*Titles in the Series*

*Campaigns from the Ground Up: State House Elections in a National Context*
John S. Klemanski, David A. Dulio, and Michael Switalski

# CAMPAIGNS FROM THE GROUND UP
## STATE HOUSE ELECTIONS IN A NATIONAL CONTEXT

### JOHN S. KLEMANSKI, DAVID A. DULIO, AND MICHAEL SWITALSKI

Paradigm Publishers
Boulder • London

Copyright © 2015 Paradigm Publishers

Published in the United States by Paradigm Publishers, 5589 Arapahoe Avenue, Boulder, Colorado 80303 USA.

Paradigm Publishers is the trade name of Birkenkamp & Company, LLC, Dean Birkenkamp, President and Publisher.

Library of Congress Cataloging-in-Publication Data

Klemanski, John S.
  Campaigns from the ground up : state house elections in a national context / John S. Klemanski, David A. Dulio, and Michael Switalski.
      pages cm. — (Pathways of politics)
  Includes bibliographical references and index.
  ISBN 978-1-61205-692-0 (pbk. : alk. paper) — ISBN 978-1-61205-755-2 (consumer ebook)
  1. Elections—United States—States. 2. State governments—United States. 3. Campaign management—United States—States. 4. Political campaigns—United States—States. I. Title.
  JK1967.K6 2014
  324.70973—dc23

                                                            2014026451

Printed and bound in the United States of America on acid-free paper that meets the standards of the American National Standard for Permanence of Paper for Printed Library Materials.

19  18  17  16  15  5  4  3  2  1

For James, Cheryl, Lisa, Aaron, Paul, Corinne, and Perry (JSK)
For Abby and Sophia (DAD)
For my wife Roma (MS)

# CONTENTS

*List of Tables and Figures*                                          *ix*

*Preface*                                                             *xi*

*Acknowledgments*                                                     *xv*

1   State House Campaigns from a National Perspective: An Overview      1

2   The Campaign Plan: Organizing a Campaign                           31

3   The Campaign Simulation: District, Electoral,
    and Candidate Research                                             47

4   The Campaign Simulation: Applying the Research                     71

5   Texas House District 144                                           97

6   Michigan House District 91                                        109

7   Virginia House of Delegates District 94                           121

8   California Assembly District 60                                    131

9   State House Campaigns in a National Context                       141

*Notes*                                                              *153*

*References*                                                         *163*

*Index*                                                              *171*

*About the Authors*                                                  *177*

# TABLES AND FIGURES

Table 1.1    Number of Elected Officials in the United States   2

Table 1.2    Social Media Use by American Adults, 2013   18

Figure 2.1   Campaign Core Team   33

Figure 3.1   Precincts in Two Hypothetical Districts   56

Table 3.1    Vote History Example for a Hypothetical State House
             District   60

Figure 3.2   Estimating Number of Votes Needed to Win (Hypothetical
             District)   63

Table 5.1    Texas at a Glance   100

Table 6.1    Michigan at a Glance   112

Table 7.1    Virginia at a Glance   125

Table 8.1    California at a Glance   135

# PREFACE

Regular, fair, and competitive elections are considered to be a foundation of modern democratic theory and practice. As such, a large portion of political science research and literature is devoted to elections and the associated topics of political participation and voter turnout, voting rights, redistricting, incumbency, and political advertising, among many others. Moreover, media coverage of elections—especially presidential elections—dominates the news in the months prior to Election Day.

This book focuses on what we consider to be an equally important element of democratic elections—the practical aspects of the political campaigns that are waged when trying to attract voter attention and support. While always important, we believe that the activities and conduct of political campaigns have become increasingly important in competitive races, especially with the expanded number of information sources provided by the Internet, the presence of a twenty-four-hour news cycle, the continued practice of the permanent campaign in the United States, and many other factors. With these dynamics in place, the effectiveness of campaign messages and the strategic choices that campaigns make have become even more crucial to the electoral success of candidates. Modern campaigns must be organized and prepared, and they must be able to use available knowledge and technology to reach voters and make sure their supporters vote on Election Day.

To help illustrate this point, this book centers on the creation of a campaign plan in a simulation setting. A campaign plan is essential to effective campaigning, as it provides a reasoned and rational place for decision making during what is typically a chaotic time—the campaign season. Without a campaign plan, a political campaign is likely to only react to events around them, spend money unwisely, stay in a defensive mode throughout the campaign, and engage in other activities that make winning less likely. As you will discover, conducting research is an important part of creating a campaign plan. There are many different kinds of research involved in creating a campaign plan, including research designed to provide insight on a district and its voters, the opponent (as well as one's own candidate), and the political environment in which the campaign will be waged (for example, is it taking place during a presidential election year, which will likely increase voter turnout?).

This volume is the offspring of *The Mechanics of State Legislative Campaigns* (Klemanski and Dulio 2006). While we continue the emphasis on campaign plans with this book, the many changes in campaigns and elections since the publication of *Mechanics* have prompted us to write a new book that accounts for these developments. Since 2006, much has happened to alter the campaign and election landscape in the United States. We elected an African American president—twice. The rise of social media has changed the ways in which campaigns raise money and communicate with supporters and potential voters. In fact, Barack Obama's social media superiority over his opponents in both 2008 and 2012 is regarded by some observers as an important reason for his victories (Rutledge 2013). Social media's potential in political campaigns appears to be almost without limit, as both a means to communicate with and mobilize supporters and as a low-cost way of raising campaign contributions.

While Twitter is often thought of as the communication playground of pop-culture celebrities, one of the most re-tweeted tweets in history was Barack Obama's "Four More Years" message after his reelection in 2012. The potential exists for this kind of technology to have great impact in state-level campaigns as well, if only because the costs are so low. While it costs thousands of dollars to air a broadcast television commercial, there is next to no cost to establishing a campaign Twitter handle or creating a campaign Facebook page. There are problems lurking in all of this potential, however. One problem is simply how difficult it is for a campaign to attract the attention of potential voters—especially in the midst of all the other social media messages and additional media and information clutter that exists. Also, campaigns must be vigilant about the content of their postings. We have included some exercises involving social media in our crisis management section in an effort to illustrate potential problems and how to respond to them.

Other changes since the publication of the *Mechanics* book in 2006 include various revisions to state election laws in many states. For example, Colorado and Washington have joined Oregon to become universal vote-by-mail states. In addition, beginning with the 2012 elections, California began using a "top-two" primary system in which candidates from all parties compete against each other in primary elections. This means two Republicans or two Democrats could compete against each other in a general election. Continued use and some expansion of election reforms, such as early in-person voting, Election Day registration, and no-excuse absentee voting, were also part of the election process in a number of states. During this same time (and especially after the 2010 elections), a number of states adopted stricter voter identification laws, requiring that voters present state-approved photo identification documents at the polls. Each of these election law changes can have an effect on how a political campaign tries to reach voters, as well as how and when voters need to be contacted and mobilized.

Another change since 2006 has been the increased spending in political campaigns. When the *Mechanics* book was published, we allotted what we now regard as somewhat limited campaign budgets to our case study simulation campaigns: $125,000 for the Texas House race, $60,000 for the North Carolina House race, and $80,000 for the Michigan state Senate campaign.

After less than 10 years, those figures seem meager. For example, it is not uncommon for a California state assembly candidate to spend over $1 million. At the federal level, several Supreme Court decisions have relaxed the restrictions on both aggregate contributions by individuals (*McCutcheon v. Federal Election Commission* 2014) and campaign spending by outside groups, especially after the US Supreme Court's 2010 *Citizens United* decision.[1] Under First Amendment protections, corporations, labor unions, and politically active nonprofit organizations may raise and spend unlimited amounts of money in a political campaign, as long as they are independent expenditures and not direct contributions to a candidate. Moreover, some of the recent campaign spending activity represents a nationalization of political money, since some outside groups that are active in state legislative races are not based in the district or state in which the campaign is being fought. Outside spending can affect a candidate's own fund-raising abilities and goals, his or her strategy and campaign message, and media strategies by all candidates.

A major goal of this book is to provide readers with the opportunity to engage in activities that are part of an actual campaign. Typically, this will require the formation of campaign teams, which will need to decide how to divide the necessary tasks associated with a campaign plan. Because we focus on state house campaigns here, the activities are more manageable than they would be in higher-level campaigns, but the lessons learned are applicable to all campaigns. Activities associated with creating a campaign plan will take readers through the analysis of a voting district and its voters, the development of a campaign message, media strategies, volunteer identification and recruitment, and the development of a campaign budget and fund-raising strategy, along with the creation of a campaign calendar.

The companion website for this book (https://paradigm.presswarehouse .com/Books/BookDetail.aspx?productID=409730) provides supplemental information on each of the highlighted campaigns. In addition, several links to government, non-government organization, and news outlet websites allow readers to explore what kinds of data are available when conducting research on an election campaign.

# ACKNOWLEDGMENTS

Since 1996, Oakland University's Department of Political Science has offered a course simply titled "Political Campaigns." This course has been taught at various times by all three coauthors of this book. The course was created to blend the theories, principles, and techniques of political campaigning with the practical application of those theories, principles, and techniques. As such, many professionals involved in campaigning or in observing and reporting on campaigns have been invited to speak to our students, including campaign managers, media consultants, public opinion pollsters, news reporters, and candidates for public office. Those who have spoken to our students are too numerous to mention here. We would like to thank everyone who has helped make the course a success. Over the years, we have also enjoyed presentations from guest speakers who took the Political Campaigns course as students and later became involved in campaigns in a variety of capacities.

We would also like to thank the Department of Political Science at Oakland University for providing support and encouragement for the Political Campaigns course and for the completion of this book. Two Oakland University political science students—Jenna Blankenship and Adam George—provided much-needed research support, collecting data on voting histories, campaign finance activities, and campaign finance laws and locating news stories on our 2012 and 2013 elections. Their assistance was invaluable to us as we prepared the manuscript for this book.

Finally, we would like to thank the students of the Oakland University Political Campaigns course over the many years it has been offered. As instructors, we have been impressed by the work accomplished by our students. We also would like to thank Paradigm Publishers and its editorial and production staff, especially vice president and associate publisher Jennifer Knerr. Many thanks to Daniel M. Shea, Pathway series editor for Paradigm Publishers, who encouraged us to write this book and offered helpful advice along the way.

# Chapter 1

# State House Campaigns from a National Perspective

## An Overview

In delivering his Gettysburg Address, President Abraham Lincoln was honoring the soldiers who had died in the Civil War and was dedicating a military cemetery at Gettysburg. In the address, however, Lincoln uttered some of the most famous words of his presidency. The speech began: "Four score and seven years ago our fathers brought forth on this continent a new nation, conceived in liberty, and dedicated to the proposition that all men are created equal." The last sentence of the speech included this: "government of the people, by the people, for the people." These words remind us of the nature of our democracy. It is incumbent upon the people to participate in government in order for it to work properly.

There are many ways Americans can become involved in their government. Professor Dan Shea and his colleagues call these avenues for participation "pathways of action." In particular, pathways are "the activities, institutions, and decision points in American politics and government that affect the creation, alteration, and preservation of laws and public policies" (Shea, Green, and Smith 2014, 14). This book is about one pathway that can help keep the United States a government "by the people." Elections are the main method we use to choose those who serve in our representative democracy, and the voting process is a large part of the elections pathway. But there are other elements to this as well.

This includes running for office, which is arguably the ultimate form of political participation.

There are over 500,000 elected officials in the United States (see Table 1.1). Each of these individuals, before they became part of government, participated in a campaign and won an election. The processes, actors, dynamics, decisions, and activities that are involved in running a successful campaign are the main theme of this book. We will demonstrate, however, that there is no single answer to the question, "How do I win an election?" Another theme of the book is that this pathway is one that is open to the public and relatively accessible to those who are interested and motivated. Moreover, candidates for elected office come to the decision to enter the fray of politics for different reasons. They may choose to run for office because of a particular issue they care deeply about, a desire to give back to their community and serve the public, a desire to make an impact on public policy, or myriad other reasons.

Michigan state Representative Collene Lamonte, whose 2012 campaign is one of four featured in this book, never thought of herself as a possible candidate before the time she decided to run for office.[1] Her pathway to elected office surprised Collene as much as anyone else. Lamonte attended Oakland University before graduating from Saginaw Valley State and becoming a high school math and science teacher in the Muskegon, Michigan, public school district. When her husband Jeff was laid off, the couple and their two young children struggled. The Lamontes lost their home to foreclosure during the housing market collapse and ended up living in Collene's mother's basement. Life's prospects looked grim.

As they fought to rebuild their financial lives, Collene grew frustrated with the state's budget cuts to K–12 schools. She saw firsthand the impact they had

**Table 1.1**   Number of Elected Officials in the United States

| Level of Government | Elected Officials |
|---------------------|-------------------|
| Federal             | 542               |
| State               | 18,828            |
| Local               | 493,830           |
| Total               | 513,200           |

Source: Christopher R. Berry and Jacob E. Gersen, "The Fiscal Consequences of Electoral Institutions," Olin Law and Economics, Working Paper no. 344, June 2007, University of Chicago Law School.

on her students and feared for the reduced opportunities her own children would have. During discussions with fellow teachers, Collene's frustration boiled over. "We have to do something!" she exclaimed. "What can we do?"

At about that same time, petitions were circulating in an attempt to recall Michigan Governor Rick Snyder (R) over education policy. Collene volunteered for the signature gathering campaign. While she had never been involved in politics before, she did not want to passively accept policies she believed were leading to lower student achievement. During the campaign, she met former state Representative Mary Valentine, who was speaking out against the cuts. Collene was starstruck. Afterwards, she felt like she had made a fool of herself, passionately describing her experiences to Valentine. Though the recall effort later fizzled, Lamonte continued to volunteer for grassroots efforts to change education policy.

Michigan's 91st District near Muskegon in western Michigan is narrowly divided between the Republican and Democratic parties and has frequently been an election battleground. Valentine's successor in the legislature, Republican Holly Hughes, had won the seat narrowly in 2010, helping Republicans capture the majority in the state House from the Democrats. During the ensuing session, Hughes supported the education cuts that Lamonte opposed.

Late in 2011, Valentine met with a group of local Democratic Party activists to begin the search for a challenger to Hughes. There seemed to be no obvious candidate willing to take on an incumbent in the swing district. After a fruitless discussion, including several unsuccessful attempts to persuade Valentine to come out of retirement and run again, the former representative offered a suggestion: "I think Collene should run."

Lamonte was stunned.

She never saw herself as a candidate. She had never been active in politics before her volunteer efforts gathering signatures on the recall petition. The idea of her running seemed preposterous. She had gone to college, gotten married, had children, and taught school. A legislator? Never. "I was simply a teacher, wife, and mother who was working to make a difference and have the voices of average, everyday people be heard," recalled Lamonte. "It became almost a David and Goliath scenario." But the group around her liked the idea. They told her that she knew the issues firsthand, had the energy and passion, was able to relate to people, and could do the job well. Besides, every once in a while, David defeats Goliath.

Collene went home, talked to her family, and entered the race. Ultimately she won a seat in the Michigan House of Representatives. She won the closest election in the state legislature in 2012, with a margin of 333 votes out of a total of over 40,000 votes cast. In the legislature, she continued to make education policy a priority.

Collene Lamonte is a clear example of an everyday American who first discovers, and then follows, her own pathway into politics. Her pathway is one that many others will duplicate. Volunteering, interning, and working on campaigns are key pathways into political participation in our democracy.

This book examines how modern campaigns for seats in state house chambers are waged. It will provide the reader with some of the basic tools necessary to create and execute an effective campaign. It will cover the many elements of running a state house campaign with an eye toward both the art and science of campaigning. While there are universal elements in any campaign and necessities that any candidate must include in their effort to win office (this is the science of campaigning), there are countless ways to conduct the campaign (this is the art).

We have chosen to focus on planning for state house races for three reasons. First, we hope to fill somewhat of a void in the information that is available on campaigns at this level, as most literature (both academic and popular) tends to emphasize higher profile federal races such as those for the US Senate, the US House of Representatives, or the presidency.

Second, considerable variation exists among the states when it comes to public policies, election laws, and political culture. You will discover many such differences among the four states we investigate in this book. Moreover, some of the more recent scholarship investigating state politics has brought to light the increasing importance of state legislative politics. For example, scholars have noted that most state legislatures wield considerable influence on national and state elections (see Dye 2000). In part this is because of policy devolution to the states that began in the 1980s and reached its height in the mid-1990s. In recent years this has continued with what some have called President Obama's "progressive federalism," which has allowed states to play a larger role in certain areas (e.g., greenhouse gas emissions and other environmental policies in California) (Schwartz 2009). In addition, state legislatures have been playing a critical role on far-reaching issues ranging from the economy in the wake of efforts to recover from the economic downturn in 2008 to social issues such as gay marriage and affirmative action. State legislatures have also played a role in the implementation of the Affordable Care Act (also known as Obamacare).

For example, some states decided to set up health care exchanges of their own, while others opted to have their residents participate in the federal exchange. In addition, some states decided to participate in the expansion of Medicaid while others did not.

Another reason for the increased importance of state legislatures has to do with their role in redistricting decisions, which can help shape the makeup of legislative bodies in each state and in Washington, DC. In most states the redistricting process—the redrawing of district borders for state house, state senate, and the US House of Representatives that takes place after each decennial census—is a political process. Usually the state legislature draws up a plan that must pass both houses and then be signed by the state's governor (exceptions include the nonpartisan/bipartisan commissions employed in Iowa and California). Because partisan officeholders usually try to help their fellow partisans, gerrymandering—drawing district lines for partisan purposes—can occur. This can have important effects on who serves in a particular body. Some observers have declared that gerrymandering in the redistricting process has greatly enhanced the partisan polarization felt in the country nationwide. Election forecaster and neuroscientist Sam Wang from Princeton University called the elections of 2012 "the Great Gerrymander," finding that gerrymandering cost Democrats 15 US House seats (Wang 2013). Political scientist Nicholas Goedert (2012) finds similar effects of redistricting on election outcomes. Others, such as Chen and Rodden (2013), Sean Trende (2013), and Abramowitz, Alexander, and Gunning (2006), are less convinced of the specific impact of redistricting. While all agree there has been a decline in the number of competitive districts, some have argued that this is because of demographic changes and ideological realignments in the United States. Despite these differences, research has found that drawing district lines has had at least some effect on election outcomes in the aggregate.[2] Even if redistricting decisions made by state legislatures only affected one or two state house or senate districts per state, that could be enough to tip majority control of those chambers to one party or the other.

The ability to make state policy in controversial areas such as those noted above, as well as policy areas that are less familiar, typically falls to the majority party in a state legislature, so establishing and maintaining a majority is crucial for both major parties. With majority party status comes considerable power both formally—through control of the chamber's schedule, leadership positions, and committee chairmanships, for example—and informally, through control of the chamber's agenda.

The third and final reason we selected state legislative campaigns is a more pragmatic one: for simulation purposes, they simply are more manageable than races for the US House—where there are over 700,000 people per district— or the US Senate—where each senator in the states included here represents between roughly 6 million (Virginia) and 38 million (California) people. The district populations in the four cases presented in later chapters are all manageable, ranging from approximately 80,000 in Virginia's 94th House of Delegates District to 161,000 in Texas's 144th State House District, and from 90,000 in Michigan's 91st State House District. Only California's 60th State Assembly District, with a population of about 470,000, is large enough to present some major challenges to a low-resource campaign organization.

## Existing Knowledge on Campaigning and Electioneering

To say that the existing academic literature on elections and campaigns is extensive is an understatement. Much of what exists, however, tends to focus on presidential campaigns or elections for the US Congress. Moreover, rather than electioneering, these works have emphasized the processes and players involved in campaigns—including a discussion of campaigns as part of a larger treatment of voter turnout and party identification, the presidential nominating process, the Electoral College, and campaign finance, to name only a few. An extensive review of this literature is beyond the scope of this book.[3]

Relatively new to the scholarly literature is a focus on how campaigns are run and on the professionals who run them. Robert Agranoff (1972) was an early voice noting a new style of political campaigning. Taking this general approach are works that have focused on the strategic component of professional political consultants' services to candidates.[4] Still others fall into a category that might be considered how-to books detailing how a candidate for a (usually) lower-level race might organize and run a campaign. Among the books in this category are *Winning Elections* (2008) by Dick Simpson, *The Campaign Manager: Running and Winning Local Elections* (2014) by Catherine Shaw, Lawrence Grey's *How to Win a Local Election* (2007), Christine Pelosi's *Campaign Boot Camp 2.0: Basic Training for Candidates, Staffers, Volunteers, and Nonprofits* (2012), and *The Victory Lab: The Secret Science of Winning Campaigns* by Sasha Issenberg (2012). More interest in the importance of the Internet and social media in campaigns is reflected in works by authors such as Colin Delany (2014). In addition to what we offer in this volume, a book that offers a good balance between theory and practice is *Campaign Craft* (2010) by Michael John Burton and Dan Shea. It provides true-to-life campaign sensibilities while reminding readers of the bigger-picture theories. Another positive feature is its emphasis on the planning needed to wage a successful campaign.

## National and Statewide Campaigns vs. Down-Ballot Races

What the average American knows about campaigns and the process of campaigning does not necessarily reflect the reality of most of the electoral contests in the United States. There are different kinds of campaigns—from president of the United States to local sheriff—and each type has its own unique characteristics. However, what we know about campaigns tends to apply only to one kind of campaign—those federal and statewide contests for the highest offices in the land. This is for good reason. The average person tends to know much more about national-level political campaigns simply because the media tends to cover them so much more. This is clearly seen every four years in the seemingly 24-hour, 7-day-a-week coverage of presidential campaigns. Also, many candidates in federal-level campaigns can afford to advertise on television and radio, so those races are much more visible to the electorate than down-ballot races (i.e., those races that are placed lower on the ballot; those at the top tend to be presidential, congressional, or gubernatorial), whose candidates usually cannot afford to buy airtime for a radio or television commercial. But the information we have about more prominent campaigns does not necessarily always apply to what happens in down-ballot elections.

The following sections illustrate some subtle (and not-so-subtle) differences, as well as similarities, that the reader may not realize exist. These factors and dynamics give an indication of how most of the campaigns in the United States compare to those with which we are most familiar but which are the least common. In this book, we deal predominantly with some of the main differences we see in national races versus local-level races that reflect how the campaigns for these offices are waged. We also note some of the similarities that occur across all types of campaigns, whether the race is for the presidency, a city council seat, a governorship, or a state house seat. In other words, all campaigns contain common elements that speak to the transferability of many of the concepts and themes we present here.

Our discussion of the differences and similarities between federal-level campaigns and state-level campaigns is centered on some of the most important and recognizable differences and similarities. The differences include, but are not limited to, media attention, salience among the electorate, voter turnout, campaign finance, campaign communication, party involvement, and outside influences.

While there are similarities, the fact remains that the types of campaigns one sees played out on television—in both media coverage and campaign advertising—are typically not like those presented in the case studies in the chapters that follow. We should note, however, that the differences that we point out between federal and statewide races and down-ballot campaigns are not either/or scenarios where one is black and the other white; rather, these differences should be viewed as gradations and matters of degree. In other words, we do not view types of races as strict categories where every race of each type nicely conforms. Rather, in the sections that immediately follow, we are describing tendencies. Some state legislative races do resemble federal and statewide campaigns, but for the most part, the differences we describe hold across various types of races.

## Media Attention

Presidential elections are arguably the most covered spectacles in American politics. Rarely do other events receive as much attention for long periods of time. Any presidential race in recent memory easily illustrates this point. Indeed, the historic 2008 election that saw the United States elect its first African American president may have been the most covered event in American history. What's more, coverage of a presidential campaign begins far in advance of what is considered the traditional campaign season. Media coverage is heavy even for potential candidates who travel to Iowa or New Hampshire two to three years before a primary election or caucus. Once the campaign gets into full swing, media coverage increases dramatically. The national media cover the primary election campaign on a daily basis, sometimes for more than a full year before any primary or caucus is held. For instance, during the 2012 presidential primary season, the first debate among Republicans seeking their party's nomination was held, and received national media coverage, on March 4, 2011, a full ten months before the first caucus and seventeen months before the nominating convention.

Everything seems to be covered during a presidential campaign—from high-profile events to matters that some would consider mundane. Coverage of debates between candidates, major policy speeches, and even strategic decisions by the campaigns are likely to be more high profile, while the details of campaign finance reports or a staff shake-up in one of the campaigns might be considered more trivial. One aspect of modern campaigns that feeds this constant coverage is the ubiquity of survey research data, or polling. The daily tracking of who is ahead and who is behind in these contests—often dubbed the "horse race"—offers up fresh data regularly for the media to provide. During the 2012 campaign, 38 percent of all coverage was devoted to the horse race; this was actually down from 2008, when it comprised 53 percent of all coverage, more than twice the amount of coverage devoted to policy stories.[5]

Interestingly, one area of presidential election coverage has actually declined: network TV coverage of the parties' national nominating conventions. Networks have chosen, in recent election years, to air their normal programming instead of what amounts to an evening infomercial for a political party and its candidates for president and vice president. In 2012, for instance, during the first night of the Republican convention, CBS showed a rerun of "Hawaii Five-O," NBC aired a new episode of "Grimm," and ABC showed an episode of "Castle" rather than showing Ann Romney, wife of presidential candidate Mitt Romney, kick off the event. Much of the convention coverage has migrated away from networks to cable TV. For example, during the 2012 conventions, the major broadcast news networks aired only three hours of coverage during each of the four-day events. This was down from four hours of coverage (one hour per night) during the 2008 conventions but the same amount as the 2004 events (Peters 2012). At their previous low point of coverage—the 2000 campaign—the major networks devoted eight and a half hours of airtime to each convention (Wayne 2001). While the recent amount of coverage is small relative to the past, this is time and attention that no other candidate for any other office in the country receives.

Gubernatorial and congressional elections receive less media attention than do presidential campaigns, but they receive much more coverage than local and state legislative campaigns. So-called earned media—which is defined as a news organization's reports of a candidate's campaign that appear in newspapers, on television, on the radio, or online—is important to any campaign since it represents exposure the campaign would not otherwise get. As with presidential contests, the coverage that is garnered in these types of races is mostly focused on the horse race. However, one important difference is that campaigns for the US House are much less likely to get television coverage than US Senate and gubernatorial races. Television news media still tend to cover US Senate campaigns, while newspapers—both print and online—are where House candidates look to attract earned media.

This is an important difference because when we move from US House campaigns to those we discuss here, the differences are just as stark. Just as House candidates have difficulty attracting earned media attention from television sources, local campaigns have trouble attracting any significant media attention from any media source. It is rare that a major news outlet in a large city will devote much coverage to the local-level races that are on the ballot. Typically, coverage of the kind of campaign discussed in this book is found only in local papers in the communities affected by the race. In some areas, these local papers are not printed at all but have moved to an entirely online presence. While this might make it easier to fit a story about a local race into the publication because there are fewer space constraints, it remains difficult because the staff is likely small at these news outlets. So, while all campaigns seek media attention, some are more successful than others, depending in large part on the kind of office being sought.

### Salience

Salience, which measures attention paid to the campaign by the public, is closely tied to media attention. Because the media devote a great deal of coverage to presidential and other high-profile races, the salience of those campaigns with the public is very high relative to other campaigns. The fact that presidential candidates are very visible—often jetting from one state to another for appearances—plays a part in the high salience of these campaigns as well. In short, presidential candidates are very visible, in part due to media attention, and that results in more Americans (and many people outside the United States) paying attention to their campaign activities.

Moreover, the issues emphasized by presidential and some senatorial and gubernatorial campaigns make potential voters stand up and take notice. The issues of the 2012 presidential campaign clearly bear this out. The economy and how to create jobs nationally, the federal deficit and debt, immigration, and President Obama's health care reform law were important to a great number of Americans. Therefore, many felt there was quite a bit at stake during the campaign for the highest office in the land. This is reflected in polling data from the 2012 election cycle. For instance, in mid-October 2012, a Pew Research Center survey showed that 66 percent of Americans said they had given "quite a lot" of thought to the presidential election, while 28 percent said they had given it "only a little" thought.[6] The proportion who indicated they had given quite a lot of thought increased to 80 percent a few days before Election Day 2012 (with only 16 percent saying "only a little").[7]

Again, a different picture emerges when we consider other types of races. Congressional races show less salience than presidential contests. In mid-October 2010, only 55 percent of Americans said they had given "quite a lot" of thought to the election, while a full 34 percent said they had given "only a little" thought to those congressional contests.[8] The interest and attention paid to elections further down the ballot only show lower levels of engagement. For instance, while a presidential campaign may focus on the differences between the candidates in terms of the economy or questions of terrorism, a state legislative campaign may be about local road conditions, the quality of the parks in the district, or other local issues. In addition, even when compared to campaigns for the US House of Representatives, many potential voters do not know how the candidates stand on the issues that are central in down-ballot campaigns (Maisel 2002).

For these reasons, candidates and campaigns for lower-level offices do not register much on the voting population's radar, even as Election Day approaches. Many voters simply consider these offices less important than those farther up the ballot. Consequently, when considering candidates for state legislative offices, many voters use traditional decision-making shortcuts (i.e., heuristics), such as selecting a candidate with a name they recognize (perhaps an incumbent, a celebrity, or someone with an ethnic-sounding name), selecting a female candidate (or specifically not), or voting by party affiliation. Therefore, party affiliation (of both voter and candidate) can be an important voting cue in elections at this level. This does not necessarily mean that the state or local party organizations are active in these campaigns or that candidates are able to rely on the party organization for assistance, but party can play a major role in determining the outcomes of state legislative races and other low-salience campaigns.

### Voter Turnout

The United States had nearly 222 million people of voting age as of the 2012 election; 23.6 million of these were in California, Texas accounted for over 16 million, 7.3 million were in Michigan, and Virginia had nearly 6 million.[9] The number of voters who actually go to the polls on Election Day, however, is far lower.

Generally speaking, voter turnout in the United States is relatively low. According to Professor Michael McDonald, a leading expert on voter turnout, the 2012 presidential election saw a turnout of about 58 percent of eligible voters; this was down from about 62 percent in 2008 and roughly 60 percent in 2004.[10] Why is there low voter turnout? That question is beyond the scope of this book,[11] but suffice it to say that there are some clear reasons, starting with the fact that many Americans, while they meet the legal requirements to be a voter, are not registered to vote and therefore cannot cast a ballot on Election Day. According to the US Census, only about 153 million people registered to vote in time for the 2012 presidential election.[12] In the states we are investigating, California had about 18,246,000 people registered in 2012, Michigan had 5,620,000, Texas had 10,479,000, and Virginia had 4,210,000.[13] Simply having individuals who are eligible but not registered to vote dampens turnout. Beyond that, nonvoters give several reasons for not going to the polls. The top four reasons Americans gave for not voting in 2012 were that they were too busy or had a conflicting schedule (18.9 percent), they were not interested (15.7 percent), they were sick or had a disability (14.0 percent), and they did not like the candidates or the campaign issues (12.7 percent).[14] There are other reasons for not voting, but being busy and not being motivated are two key issues, even in a presidential election.

In addition, voter turnout varies across election years. It is highest in presidential election years and drops substantially in midterm elections. Turnout in the 2006 and 2010 midterm elections was roughly 41 percent. The main difference between presidential and midterm years is simply that there is no presidential contest to attract voters' attention and drive turnout. Some states employ odd-numbered-year elections—holding contests during years when there is neither a presidential nor a congressional election. New Jersey and Virginia are two notable states that have governor's races in odd-numbered years; many US municipalities also hold mayoral races in odd years—all a result of the Progressive Era reforms of the early 1900s. The statewide turnout in New Jersey for the 2013 governor's race was less than 40 percent, while in Virginia turnout was over 42 percent. Smart campaigners recognize what type of election year in which they are operating and devise a strategy based on the number of voters expected to go to the polls (see Chapters 2 and 3 for more on this).

Turnout can also differ within election years. In short, more people cast ballots for the races at the top of the ticket—those for president, or in midterm years governor, US Senate, or even US House if there is no gubernatorial or Senate contest. As voters go down the ballot, there often occurs what is referred to as "ballot roll-off," where voters stop voting. Take for instance, one area in Michigan. In 2012, a total of 55,982 votes were cast in the race for the 40th State House District seat. Compare this to races further up the ballot like those for the presidency and the US Senate, which, in the same precincts that make up the 40th District, saw vote totals of 72,432 and 71,150, respectively. The state House race did not see the lowest vote totals, as the total number of votes cast in the Michigan Supreme Court race was 54,307.[15] Indeed, ballot roll-off in low-salience state supreme court races typically is 20–30 percent (Bonneau and Hall 2009). Roll-off unquestionably impacts campaign strategies because in down-ballot races fewer votes are needed to win on Election Day. While this may seem like good news for campaigners, these votes may be harder to identify than the votes in a presidential or senatorial contest.

Voter turnout, in one sense, helps determine the outcome of the election. Under the electoral rules in the United States, the winner of the election is the one with the most votes.[16] In a two-person race, campaigners can estimate the votes they need to win by predicting voter turnout and simply taking a majority of those votes as their vote goal. It is paramount that a campaign know how to estimate how many voters will turn out on Election Day, and more importantly whether their supporters are making it to the polls. This is arguably even more important in down-ballot races, where turnout is lower and fewer votes are needed to win. Turning out one more voter might mean the difference between winning and losing.

One way to track who is turning out is having volunteers at the polls on Election Day. Since the inception of absentee voting—which originally allowed voters who were going to be away from their voting precinct on Election Day to cast a ballot by mail—campaigns have been able to track these votes. With absentee votes, campaigns could track who had requested and returned an absentee ballot. More recent innovations—including loosening the requirements for requesting an absentee ballot; creating opportunities for voters to cast a ballot early such as early in-person voting; and more and more voters opting for what is termed "no excuse" absentee voting—make tracking who has voted more difficult for campaigns. This is especially true for campaigns in down-ballot races that mainly rely on volunteers. In 2012, Texas saw about 40 percent of its voters vote before Election Day,[17] while over 51 percent of voters in California voted early.[18] In addition to absentee voting and voting by mail, more than thirty states (including Texas and California) offer early in-person voting, which allows voters to vote at selected polling places on one of several days, usually about two weeks prior to Election Day.[19] In Texas, for instance, voters may show up at a polling place beginning seventeen days prior to Election Day. In effect, this creates seventeen election days in Texas. Again, in down-ballot races, this puts a strain on a small campaign operation with few volunteers.

## Campaign Finance

The amounts of money campaigns at the top of the ticket versus those down the ballot are able to raise and spend may be the most significant difference between high-level and down-ballot races. However, the similarity here is that all campaigns, irrespective of the office being sought, need to raise money to be successful. But spending differences between these races are stark, and they have important consequences for how campaigns are run at different levels.

Presidential campaigns are clearly the most well-funded campaigns in the United States. In large part this is because these campaigns must cover the most ground and speak to the greatest number of people. In 2008, Barack Obama shattered the record for money raised and spent in a presidential race—roughly $750 million. In 2012, President Obama failed to duplicate this fund-raising level, but he came close with $715 million. His opponent in 2012, Republican Mitt Romney, raised and spent nearly $450 million.[20]

Candidates running for the US House of Representatives, the US Senate, or another statewide office do not spend as much as presidential candidates, but they do raise and spend substantial amounts in most cases. The amount a candidate raises and spends when running for US Congress is often driven by the competitiveness of the race. According to the Campaign Finance Institute, sitting senators running for reelection (i.e., incumbents) who won reelection with more than 60 percent of the vote (i.e., they won by more than 20 percentage points) spent more than $7 million on average in 2012; the challenger candidates who opposed them spent less than $1.5 million. Those incumbent senators who won with less than 60 percent of the vote spent nearly $12.8 million, while those who ran against them spent over $10 million. In 2012, one incumbent senator was defeated—Scott Brown, a Republican from Massachusetts. He spent over $35 million in his reelection effort, only to lose to Democrat Elizabeth Warren, who spent over $42 million.[21] Similarly, incumbent members of the House who won by a margin of more than 20 percentage points in 2012 spent $1.3 million on average; challenger candidates who opposed them spent only about $150,000. Incumbents who won with less than 60 percent of the vote spent over $2.2 million on average in 2012; the candidates who ran against these incumbents spent on average nearly $1 million. And in races where an incumbent was defeated in his or her attempt to return to the House, the average incumbent spent over $3 million, while the challengers who defeated them spent nearly $2.5 million.[22] One of the incumbents who lost, Allen West (R-FL 18), spent over $18 million.

Why do campaigns cost so much? In the modern reality of electioneering, candidates for the US House and Senate demand and employ many of the same tactics and tools that are used by presidential candidates. The funds in congressional campaigns rise to these levels for several reasons. First, they are spent simply to employ modern campaign tactics (e.g., television ads and sophisticated direct mail campaigns). Second, these candidates are communicating with a large number of potential voters. As noted above, US House members represent over 700,000 people each, and US Senators represent anywhere between roughly 580,000 (Wyoming) and 38 million (California) people. Different candidates spend large sums of money for different reasons. One may ask: Why does a candidate who wins by more than 60 percent of the vote need to spend so much when the election outcome is not in question? Very simply, those who win by a large margin spend large sums because they do not want to take any chances. Richard Fenno noted in his seminal work on how US House members relate to their constituents that incumbents never feel safe in their districts and are always working to ensure reelection (Fenno 1978). Candidates who are in competitive races—those who win *and* those who lose—spend what they believe they must in order to win the election. This often simply entails more of everything—more television commercials, more mail, more phone calls, more polling, and so forth. Not all candidates spend large sums, however. Clearly, candidates who raise little and have a slim chance of winning do not spend a lot. But even candidates who win can spend small amounts (relative to the figures above). For instance, US Representative Jose E. Serrano (D-NY 15) spent only about $200,000 in his successful effort to win reelection in 2012, and Senator Angus King (I-ME) spent less than $3 million to win his US Senate seat in the same year.[23]

Similar patterns of spending are found in state legislative races. Many candidates spend large sums, but others do not. For instance, during the 2012 election cycle in the state of Texas, one candidate—Joe Stauss (R) in House District 121—raised over $6.5 million in a race where he faced only token opposition in the general election. In District 78, Don Margo (R) raised over $800,000 in a losing bid to retain his seat. The eventual winner in the 78th District was Joe Moody (D), who raised less than $500,000. That said, the average candidate running for state house in Texas in 2012 raised $194,000.[24]

Ron Reynolds (D), in District 27, raised less than $45,000 in his winning campaign. The average assembly candidate in California raised more than $318,000, with one candidate, Democrat Ken Cooley, raising more than $4 million in his effort to defeat Peter Tateishi (R), who raised over $1 million, in the 8th District. But in an open seat race in District 36, the two candidates raised less than $430,000 combined in their campaigns, with the winner raising only about $320,000.

There is no doubt that campaign spending in the United States is on the rise—more and more is spent each election cycle at all levels of campaigning. According to one estimate, spending in state and local elections increased from $465 million in 1980 (all races) to over $1 billion in the 1996 elections (Maisel 2002, chap. 11). The National Institute on Money in State Politics finds that between 2000 and 2012, the total funds raised by all candidates in state-level races went from less than $1.5 billion to over $2.75 billion. The Center for Responsive Politics reports that over the same period the total cost of US federal elections increased from just over $3 billion to over $6.3 billion.[25]

There are two other important points about campaign finance that any student of campaigns and elections should know. First, there are only five basic sources from which candidates can raise campaign funds. Candidates at all levels may accept contributions from individual citizens, political parties, certain types of political action committees (PACs), and in some instances other candidates. Candidates may also contribute to their own campaign. Second, direct contributions to candidates are heavily regulated. There are many rules about how much each entity can contribute to a candidate and what must be reported to the government by both contributors and candidates who accept the contributions. At the federal level during the 2013–2014 election cycle, individuals could contribute $2,600 to a candidate, PACs could contribute $5,000, a party organization $5,000, and another candidate $2,000 per election.[26] As one might expect, there is significant variation in contribution limits across states, which is driven by the great variation in campaign finance laws across states. For instance, some states have very low individual contribution limits, while other states allow unlimited contributions. PAC contribution limits also vary greatly, from small dollar amounts to unlimited amounts. Moreover, contribution limits can vary depending on the office for which the candidate is running.[27] In Michigan state House races, individuals can only contribute $1,000 per election (they can give $2,000 to state Senate candidates and $6,800 to gubernatorial candidates); independent PACs can contribute $10,000; and state parties can give $10,000.[28] In California the contribution limits are $3,900 per election for individuals and $7,800 for PACs, and there are no limits on political party contributions.[29] If someone is going to run a campaign in any state, one of the first pieces of information to gather is how much the different entities can legally contribute to the campaign.

## Campaign Communication

All types of campaigns need to communicate with potential voters. Each campaign will (or should) have a clear and consistent message it will disseminate to those they hope will vote for them on Election Day. However, there are major differences in how campaigns at different levels communicate and in the tools they use to do so.

Again, presidential campaigns are the most familiar example because that is what Americans see the most. As we noted above, these are very well covered by the media, and many Americans see a lot of television commercials during a campaign. During the 2012 campaign, Barack Obama and Mitt Romney each spent over $400 million delivering their message to voters on broadcast and cable television.[30] Television is also a very important tool in campaigns for governor and US Senate. For statewide elections, television is simply an efficient way of reaching a lot of voters. Television ads are generally placed in media markets that cover major metropolitan areas. Media markets are not always consistent with political boundaries, but they generally fit within state borders. To advertise statewide, a campaign may have to buy broadcast airtime in several different media markets. For instance, to advertise statewide in a gubernatorial race in Virginia, a candidate would have to buy airtime in five Virginia media markets—Charlottesville, Harrisonburg, Norfolk-Portsmouth-Newport News, Richmond-Petersburg, and Roanoke-Lynchburg—as well as the Washington, DC, media market, which covers northern Virginia. It is expensive, but viable candidates for these offices are able to raise the requisite funds for blanketing the airwaves across a state or the nation.

Candidates in national and statewide races also use other forms of communication. One of these is direct mail, which can take many forms, including letters, postcards, and brochures. One important benefit of direct mail is that it can be targeted with pinpoint messages the candidate wants a particular segment of the electorate to see. Often referred to as microtargeting, this method can direct very specific messages to potential voters based on their personal characteristics.

In addition, some campaigns have begun using sophisticated telephone calling programs that send recorded messages (known as robocalls) to targeted members of the electorate, often featuring the voice of a famous individual or someone who will get the attention of the person being called. In short, a wide variety of techniques are used by candidates in high-level races to communicate the messages they want the voting public to hear.

One of the most recent innovations in campaigning is the leveraging of technology offered by the Internet and social media in particular. Once again, presidential campaigns have led the way. In the early days of Internet campaigning, candidates used their campaign website as little more than a digital yard sign (Casey 1996). However, its use quickly expanded to fund-raising, with John McCain and Howard Dean setting records in 2000 and 2004, respectively. The largest leap in utilizing the Internet was seen in Barack Obama's presidential campaigns in 2008 and 2012. In 2008, the Obama campaign created its own social media environment with MyBarackObama.com, or MyBO. The site was modeled after Facebook, and the campaign hired Facebook cofounder Chris Hughes to help develop the technology. The Obama campaign stepped up its efforts in 2012, leveraging social media technology to collect vast amounts of data on potential voters that they used to contact supporters and help turn them out on Election Day (Romano 2012). The Pew Research Center has been tracking Internet and social media use over the years, and its findings suggest a great deal of potential for political campaigns to communicate with voters through the Internet and social media (see Table 1.2). In addition to the social media use data reported in Table 1.2, a 2014 survey found

**Table 1.2**   Social Media Use by American Adults, 2013

| Social Media Site | Percentage |
|-------------------|------------|
| Facebook          | 71         |
| LinkedIn          | 22         |
| Pinterest         | 21         |
| Twitter           | 18         |
| Instagram         | 17         |

Source: Maeve Duggan and Aaron Smith, "Social Media Update 2013," Pew Research Internet Project, December 30, 2013, http://www.pewinternet.org/2013/12/30/social-media-update-2013.

that 87 percent of American adults use the Internet, up from only 14 percent in 1995.[31] Moreover, the Pew survey found that 74 percent of online adults use at least one social networking site, while 42 percent use multiple sites.[32]

Candidates in down-ballot races also use various approaches to reach potential voters. However, the techniques and tactics are very different from those used in high-level campaigns. In down-ballot races, television advertising is rare. In these races, candidates are often running in a relatively small segment of a media market. This makes broadcast television inefficient because the ads would be seen by many individuals who are not in the candidate's district and could not vote for him or her even if they wanted to. Cable television, however, is an option in down-ballot races if the campaign is well funded. It still takes a sizable budget to produce a quality television ad and purchase airtime, but buying airtime on local cable systems makes sense for some candidates in state house races. This can be an efficient use of resources, since many cable systems will bundle airtime purchases for political ads so that the ads air on multiple channels watched by likely voters—those with lots of news programming, for example.

In most down-ballot races, direct mail is a likely electioneering communication tool. The same benefits that presidential and gubernatorial candidates obtain from targeted mail—messages tailored to specific groups of individuals, for instance—are available to candidates in down-ballot races. Candidates in down-ballot races also turn to less expensive methods of communication such as door-to-door canvassing and leafleting, literature drops, and speeches before groups of potential voters.

In addition, candidates at all levels can use social media and the Internet. A candidate for city council, prosecutor, or state house is unlikely to create their own social media platform like MyBO, but they can use Facebook, Twitter, Instagram, Tumblr, YouTube, and other tools of the social media age. In part, what makes these technology-driven tactics available to candidates down the ballot is the low cost. It is nearly free to set up and maintain a Facebook page or Twitter handle. All a candidate needs is a savvy volunteer or staff person to manage the work. Moreover, the benefits of using these tactics are important no matter what level of campaign one is running. The clearest benefits are in campaign organization. Although the evidence is mixed on the usefulness of online tools in persuading voters to cast a ballot for a particular candidate (see Towner and Dulio 2011; Towner 2013), the power of social networking sites and campaign websites to organize campaign volunteers, spread information among supporters, and raise funds is clear. In down-ballot races where volunteers are the main labor force and do much of the work paid staff do in other campaigns, this kind of organizational tool can be very beneficial to candidates.

## Role of Parties

Political parties can wear many hats in campaigns, from recruiters of candidates to providers of electioneering services (Herrnson 1988; 2012). The role and impact of parties, at all levels of campaigns and with regard to electioneering, has changed substantially over time (Herrnson 1988; Aldrich 2011; Dulio 2004). While some argue that parties have surged in relevance in recent years, the fact remains that the organizations that are traditionally thought to be at the center of parties are much less involved in campaigns than they were at the height of their power (Herrnson 1988; 2004; see also Sorauf 1994; Kayden and Mahe 1985; Menefee-Libey 2000).

Even today, parties engage in different activities with varying degrees of effort at different levels of campaigns. Consider only three examples—simple organization, provision of services, and candidate recruitment—to see the differences between what parties do in different types of elections. The easiest identifiable difference between the federal level and the local level is simple organization. Elements of the national parties today—the Republican National Committee (RNC), the Democratic National Committee (DNC), and their campaign committees focused on each chamber of Congress, the Democratic Congressional Campaign Committee (DCCC), the National Republican Campaign Committee (NRCC), the Democratic Senatorial Campaign Committee (DSCC), and the National Republican Senatorial Committee (NRSC)—are very well organized, very well funded, and very active on a year-round basis. Each of these organizations has dozens of staff members working in different divisions—political, communication, press, research, fund-raising, and so forth—all with the goal of helping candidates at the federal level win elections. In 2012 the DNC raised over $316 million, while its counterpart at the presidential level, the RNC, raised over $409 million; at the US House level, the DCCC raised nearly $184 million while the NRCC raised almost $156 million; and those organizations focused on the US Senate, the DSCC and NRSC, raised $146 and $117 million, respectively.[33]

In contrast, at the state and local level there is great variation in how well organized the party apparatus is (Gray, Hanson, and Kousser 2013; Hershey 2014). For instance, some state parties are more sophisticated than others—some have part-time staff and some have full-time staff, some have large budgets while others do not, and some are active year-round while others are only operational during the election season.[34] State parties also vary in how much money they raise. Some are excellent fund-raisers. The California Democratic Party, for example, raised over $27 million during the 2012 election cycle. In Florida, the state GOP raised over $29 million. In Ohio, both parties raised roughly $15 million. Other state parties, like those in Vermont, Wyoming, Nebraska, and Mississippi, raised very little in that election year; each party raised less than $300,000, with some significantly below that figure.[35] At the local level, the variation in party strength is even more dramatic. While most counties in the United States have a party organization that has formal rules and a slate of officers, how active they are and the size of their budget will likely vary a great deal.

In the modern era, most federal political campaigns are considered to be "candidate centered" as opposed to "party centered" (Salmore and Salmore 1989; Wattenberg 1992; Menefee-Libey 2000). This means that candidates running for office at higher levels tend to rely less on political party organizations for financial and other campaign-related assistance. In addition, candidates' appeals to voters tend to focus on their own attributes and qualifications rather than their party affiliation. In short, more candidates today typically make an appeal to voters by selling their candidacy rather than their affiliation with a particular party. That said, one's political party affiliation remains the best predictor of an individual's vote choice. For instance, exit polls from the 2012 presidential election show that 92 percent of voters who called themselves Democrats voted for Obama and 93 percent of Republicans voted for Romney.[36]

In the area of providing electioneering services, important differences again appear between types of races. During the 1980s, the national party committees began to offer services to their candidates for the US House and Senate, ranging from assistance with the production of television ads and direct mail pieces to polling data and fund-raising assistance (Herrnson 1988). Today's party organizations help candidates obtain the services that they demand and need, but they hire outside professional political consultants to provide or perform the services rather than provide them in house (Dulio 2004; Kolodny and Dulio 2003). This is possible due to the large budgets with which these organizations have to work, as noted above. Again, a much different picture emerges at the state and local levels, where electioneering resembles old-style campaigning. If a state political party organization is strong and active, it may target up to ten or fifteen legislative races each year, with the hope of capturing open seats, defeating a vulnerable incumbent, or taking or retaining the majority of legislative seats.

It is to those few races that state and local party organizations tend to allocate their scarce financial and volunteer resources. Because most "local candidates cannot afford the cost of modern campaigning," including television or radio ads and survey research, the local party helps candidates by focusing on volunteers at the local precinct levels (Maisel 2002, 71).

Political parties have found ways to continually adapt and become more involved in elections. What defines a political party is changing. Some have begun to look at parties as networks of organizations that include traditional organizational structures but also organizations outside of that traditional structure (Skinner, Masket, and Dulio 2012). Organizations like super PACs, which often have former party operatives on their staff and party donors as contributors, now supplement what political parties do for candidates. As we discuss in the next section, these entities raise and spend tremendous sums during elections trying to impact the outcome of races all over the nation. When viewed as networks of the traditional structures and outside groups, parties are influential organizations.

While political parties used to be the sole gatekeepers determining which candidates would run in a general election, the amount of candidate recruitment done by parties today is relatively minimal. During the period of American politics when political parties were most powerful (especially during the late 1800s when party machines were dominant), political parties tightly controlled the selection of candidates. The party boss, the individual who ran the party, would hand-pick candidates. Thanks in large part to the work of the Progressives, a group of reformers who wanted to take power from the party bosses and give it to the rank-and-file party members, this influence largely disappeared. Because of the adoption of the direct primary, which allowed citizens to choose who would represent the party in the general election, the party power of candidate selection was taken away. After the Progressive Era, candidates could more easily recruit themselves into running for office rather than being selected to run by the party boss. Primaries are now the central mechanism for choosing candidates to run in the general election at all levels of office.[37]

When it comes to primaries, differences exist between types of races, but it is mainly presidential primaries that differ from all other types of races. Primary contests for just about every office other than the presidency are one-day affairs where voters go to the polls and vote for their favorite candidate among the other Republicans or Democrats on the ballot. Some states have adopted a different type of primary structure where rather than being categorized as Democrats and

Republicans on two ballots, all the candidates are listed together on one ballot; the top two vote getters, regardless of party affiliation, advance to the general election (see Chapter 8 for more on this topic). Presidential primaries, in contrast, are a phenomenon unlike any other in American politics. Rather than taking place on one primary election day, presidential primaries are clearly an extended process. Over the course of roughly the first six months of the presidential election year, each party in each state holds a nominating contest where voters in that state are able to register their preferences regarding who they want to be their party's nominee for the general election. Thus, presidential primary contenders must develop a strategy to compete in a number of elections, not just one.[38]

Because candidates self-select into running for office, the primary field can be quite crowded. This is most noticeable in presidential contests. For instance, in 2008, when the presidency was an open seat because President George W. Bush was term limited and Vice President Dick Cheney was not seeking the presidency, the field of candidates in both major parties was large. On the Democratic side it included at least eight candidates: Senators Barack Obama (IL), Hillary Clinton (NY), Joe Biden (DE), and Chris Dodd (CT); former Senators John Edwards (NC) and Mike Gravel (AK); US Representative Dennis Kucinich (OH 10); and former New Mexico Governor Bill Richardson. The Republican field included Senator John McCain (AZ), former New York City Mayor Rudy Giuliani, former Arkansas Governor Mike Huckabee, former Massachusetts Governor Mitt Romney, former Senator Fred Thompson (TN), former US Ambassador Alan Keyes, and US Representatives Duncan Hunter (CA 52) and Ron Paul (TX 14). In 2012, with Barack Obama running for reelection, there was only a contested Republican primary, which included Mitt Romney, Ron Paul, former US Senator Rick Santorum (PA), US Representative Michele Bachmann (MN 6), former US Ambassador Jon Huntsman, Texas Governor Rick Perry, and businessman Herman Cain. Again, because of self-selection, candidates determine whether they are going to run regardless of the wishes of the party leadership. In some instances, the party would prefer that a candidate did not run. Reaching back to their past, the party would prefer to pick the candidate themselves and avoid a contested election completely. In a hotly contested primary, the primary combatants may attack each other so that whoever wins is damaged heading into the general election. Anointing a party-favored candidate would make the whole election run more smoothly.

Many candidates for the US House and Senate are longtime party loyalists who have served as an elected official in some lower office prior to running for federal office. These individuals may be recruited by their state, congressional district, or local party organization. In targeted races that appear to be competitive, even the party's national committee leadership may be active in identifying and contacting an individual to run for office, usually with the promise of party support. Recruiting candidates to run is easier in some cases than others. A case in point is the different experiences Democrats and Republicans had in recruiting candidates to run for Michigan's open US Senate seat in 2014 after longtime Senator Carl Levin (D) decided to retire. Early on, national Democrats approached US Representative Gary Peters (MI 14) to run for the seat, and he announced his decision to enter the race on May 1, 2013 (nineteen months before the 2014 general election). No other establishment Democrat entered the primary race, allowing Democrats to coalesce around Peters, avoiding a bloody primary campaign, and allowing Peters to raise money for the general election campaign. Republicans, on the other hand, saw a number of their early target candidates decline to run for the seat, including US Representatives Justin Amash (MI 3), Dave Camp (MI 4), Mike Rogers (MI 8), and Candice Miller (MI 10); Lieutenant Governor Brian Calley; Attorney General Bill Schuette; former Attorney General Mike Cox; former gubernatorial candidate Dick DeVos; and Scott Romney, brother of former GOP presidential candidate Mitt Romney. Former Secretary of State Terri Lynn Land finally entered the race a month after Peters had announced.

The same self-selection process occurs in down-ballot races, which can result in crowded primary fields there as well. However, at this level, the party has retained more of its recruitment function (Brewer and Maisel 2012). Especially in local partisan elections, it is important for the party organization to fill the open slots in their area with quality candidates. However, this is not the case with all local party organizations. State-level legislators in many states operate on a part-time basis, and they usually have a career that offers some flexibility that allows this kind of public service. This, along with the self-selection aspect of getting into the race, allows for many candidates to follow their own pathway to the campaign. As such, many state legislators are lawyers, teachers, retirees, homemakers, and students (Moncrief, Squire, and Jewell 2000).

In states with term limits, careerism has faded substantially, especially in those states that have lifetime limits on public service across all offices. This can make it even more important for parties to engage in recruitment. With greater turnover because of term limits, there are fewer incumbents running, so the parties have more work to do filling out the ballots. In some cases it is difficult for the party to even find a candidate willing to run. This is especially true of someone who will run against an incumbent (Moncrief, Squire, and Jewell 2000). Even if the party can convince someone to run, these candidates may only put up token opposition, failing to raise much money or do much in the way of communicating with voters, and in the end, winning few votes.

### Other Outside Influences

Similarities and differences exist across other dimensions of campaigns. Modern political campaigns are not just about candidates providing voters a choice of who should take a seat in government. As we noted above, parties have an interest, as one would expect, in which candidate wins an election, and they play a role in determining who wins by way of their involvement during the campaign. But there are other entities that get involved in modern campaigns. As we noted above, PACs are major players in campaigns, as they contribute hundreds of millions of dollars to candidates each election cycle.

Since the early 1900s, it has been illegal for corporations (and labor unions since the 1940s) to make direct contributions to candidates for office.[39] But in the period after the 1970s, these organizations could create legally separate PACs to raise voluntary contributions for campaign purposes. These PACs provide a way for corporations, unions, and other outside interests to become involved in campaigning. Their roots are in the 1974 amendments to the Federal Election Campaign Act, which allowed for "multi-candidate" committees to provide contributions (limited to $5,000) to candidates for office. PACs are required to be legally separate from their corporate, union, or interest group parent organization. For instance, the Chamber of Commerce cannot give political contributions directly; its PAC, the Chamber of Commerce of the United States of America PAC, may do so. The same is true for a union like the International Brotherhood of Electrical Workers or an interest group like Planned Parenthood: Only the groups' PACs, the International Brotherhood of Electrical Workers PAC and the Planned Parenthood Federal PAC, can make direct contributions to candidates. PACs can also be "non-connected" and exist on their own without any ties to a parent organization.

In addition to making direct contributions to candidates, PACs can make what are known as independent expenditures during a campaign. These are expenditures that are made by a PAC to influence a campaign without the knowledge of the candidate. In other words, the PAC is acting independently of the candidate. Many times these independent expenditures are used to purchase television advertising time, send out direct mail pieces, or communicate the PAC's own message to potential voters. This activity is so pervasive in some races that candidate campaigns find it hard to communicate their own message in the midst of the work of outside groups that have gotten involved (Thurber 2001).

According to the Center for Responsive Politics, PACs raised a total of $1.4 billion during the 2012 federal elections. Of this total, roughly $453 million was contributed to candidates and the other $1 billion was spent on other campaign activities.[40] While PACs can become very active in campaigns such as those for the US Congress, they are much less active in down-ballot races for the state legislature. However, when PACs do get involved in contests farther down the ballot, many times they get involved at a high level. PACs can be major players in selected races at the state legislative level, many times with an eye toward impacting which party controls the majority in a legislative chamber. State-level PACs tend to adopt one of two strategies when supporting state legislative candidates: (1) PACs have tended to give more money to incumbents and other likely eventual winners because they have adopted a strategy that seeks to assure access to lawmakers; and (2) those PACs considered to be ideological (e.g., Right to Life or Planned Parenthood) have tended to support challengers or participate in competitive races more than the corporate and labor PACs (McKay 2010).

PACs, however, are only one way interest groups can become involved in campaigns. Most of the other options fall into the category of 501(c) organizations. According to the Internal Revenue Service, there are nearly thirty different classifications of 501(c) organizations, a few of which are relevant here. For example, 501(c)(3) organizations are charitable or religious groups that are forbidden from getting involved in federal campaigns and elections. These groups cannot endorse candidates, contribute to candidates, or organize a PAC. They can, however, do research and conduct "educational" activities. There also are 501(c)(4) organizations, which are nonprofit social welfare or civic advocacy organizations. These groups are allowed to become involved in politics as long as it is not the group's primary purpose. These groups can do such things as rate candidates and make independent expenditures. Finally, 501(c)(5) groups are labor, agricultural, and horticultural organizations, while 501(c)(6) groups are business leagues, chambers of commerce, and real estate boards. These groups are forbidden from making expenditures or contributions in connection with a federal election. They can, however, make independent expenditures, and they may engage in "internal communications" with members (communications with members, stockholders, and their families but not the general public).

A recent yet incredibly important change in the context of how outside groups get involved in campaigns came out of two Supreme Court decisions—*Citizens United v. Federal Election Commission* and *SpeechNow v. Federal Election Commission*. The main effect of these decisions was to allow corporations and unions to spend unlimited amounts on elections by ruling that the same First Amendment protections that allow citizens to spend unlimited amounts of money on elections also apply to independent expenditures made by corporations, unions, and other entities. The *SpeechNow* case led to the creation of a new kind of political committee—so-called super PACs.

Super PACs are "independent-expenditure-only" committees; in other words, they may not make direct contributions to candidates. These groups may accept unlimited contributions and make unlimited expenditures aimed at electing or defeating candidates for federal office. Super PACs have the same reporting requirements as traditional PACs—they must disclose both receipts and disbursements. Specifically, they have to regularly provide information on the totals they receive in contributions and what they make in expenditures, information about donors (for contributions of $200 or more), and information about each expenditure ($200 and above), including the purpose of the disbursement. Super PACs must also report information about the independent expenditures they make, which are separate from the regular reporting of disbursements. Any independent expenditure over $10,000 must be reported to the Federal Election Commission within 48 hours and must include the name of the candidate and whether the expenditure supported or opposed the candidate.

Super PACs came under heavy criticism in the first few years they were active. Some observers still have great concern that super PACs can hide their sources of funds. While super PACs have to disclose donors, these donors may be trade associations or other groups that themselves take donations but do not have the same reporting requirements, in which case the original sources of funding are still hidden.

Super PACs have become major players in federal elections. The Center for Responsive Politics reports that during the 2012 election cycle, these groups spent nearly $610 million.[41] Much of this was dedicated to the presidential race, but millions more were spent on US Senate and House races. Senate races in Ohio, Florida, Texas, Indiana, Virginia, and Wisconsin all saw more than $10 million of super PAC spending, while House races in Ohio (16th District), Illinois (8th), and Florida (18th) all saw roughly $5 million (Garrett 2013). Super

PACs are also active in state-level campaigns but with significantly fewer dollars. The National Institute on Money in State Politics notes that super PACs raised nearly $37 million for races at the state level in 2010 (Quist 2012).

In addition to making contributions to parties and candidates, outside groups may become involved in high-level campaigns by providing certain services for candidates. One of the most important and most visible of these activities falls in the category of voter mobilization, or get-out-the-vote (GOTV) efforts near Election Day. For example, labor unions are a major player for Democratic candidates in this area.

The influence of outside groups is one area where higher-level and local campaigns can be similar. While outside groups such as labor unions and other interest groups are not likely to enter the fray of a state house campaign by buying airtime for a television commercial, they may produce a piece of literature to try and communicate to potential voters, who will decide the outcome of the election. Many groups, such as labor unions, do get involved in GOTV activities close to Election Day.

### General Electioneering Principles

Some of the differences between races for president, governor, and seats in the US House and Senate and those for offices that are more local in nature should be clear. Just a few of the areas we highlighted here are that federal and statewide races are characterized by larger amounts of money, greater amounts of media coverage, higher levels of voter turnout, a different mix of communication techniques, and a greater role for political parties and other outside influences. Put another way, races for federal and statewide offices have fully adapted to the "new style" kind of campaigning Agranoff (1972) noticed four decades ago. Public opinion polling, television advertising, sophisticated fund-raising appeals, and the presence of professional political consultants who can provide all the services a campaign demands are all staples in these high-level races. Professor David M. Farrell (1996) labels these kinds of campaigns "capital intensive" and contrasts them with those that are "labor intensive." Modern campaigns for down-ballot races such as those for state legislature, city council, mayor, and county commissioner tend to be more labor intensive.

Yet there are also similarities. Candidates in down-ballot races must raise money, communicate with voters, engage in field research, and pursue other campaign activities performed at higher levels. Down-ballot campaigns are normally characterized by shoe leather activities (i.e., door-to-door canvassing and literature drops) rather than television commercials and by the use of volunteers rather than paid professional consultants. In many cases, down-ballot campaigns are comprised of little more than the candidate and a couple volunteers. One of the lessons of campaign planning is that it is even more important for campaigns with few resources to have a solid campaign plan in place before the campaign begins. Only with such a plan in place is an efficient use of resources possible—which is important when only three or four people are running a political campaign by themselves.

## Conclusion

In the chapters that follow, we guide the reader through information that describes, and exercises that illustrate, the kinds of decisions that a candidate (or a campaign manager) running in a state house race must make. The activities included resemble those that would be completed when formulating a plan on how to win the election. As readers move through the rest of this book, they will confront some of the same choices and assessments that candidates in four actual campaigns had to make.

We have chosen four cases—one each from Texas, Michigan, Virginia, and California—based on a series of factors that vary across the four districts. These factors include different regions of the country; legislatures that are full-time and part-time; states that have term limits and those that do not; different campaign finance regulations; varying lengths of the general election period (i.e., dates of the primary election differ in these states); districts that are a mixture of urban, suburban, and rural populations; and size and complexity of the district. In short, we selected the cases so that the reader would be presented with a wide variety of races and contexts in which to take on the tasks we include in the chapters that follow.

For example, the heterogeneity or homogeneity of districts will pose different challenges to campaign teams as they attempt to identify campaign issues and messages that appeal to their respective voting populations. An additional benefit of these differing districts is that by comparing the different political contexts and climates of the races, the reader will see that campaigning is as much an art as it is a science. In other words, what works in one district may not work in another. There is not a formula *per se* for campaigning that can be transferred from campaign to campaign. However, one constant across each of the four races we present is that they were all competitive in 2012 or 2013. We were careful to select races that were in competitive districts for the elections investigated because one or two wrong decisions in these campaigns could make the difference on Election Day. Also, it is simply not as much fun to simulate a campaign where the outcome is all but assured.

In each of the chapters that offer material on specific house districts, we present some general background information on the states and districts so the reader can become familiar with the context in which they would be working if they were actually participating in the race. We also provide some information that the candidate (or campaign manager) would likely collect in their efforts to put together a plan to run their campaign. The material we present in each of the case chapters is public information available to the average person—it is boilerplate material to which any campaign would want access. However, we do not necessarily provide all the information you will need to complete all of the exercises in the simulation. As will become clear, sometimes half the battle of planning how to win a race is doing the research that is necessary to create an effective strategy.

Before we introduce you to the case chapters that contain the information for the simulation, Chapter 2 will illustrate some of the principles of developing a campaign plan that can lead to victory on Election Day. In Chapters 3 and 4, we present a guide to the simulation and a series of exercises that simulate what a campaign team would undertake during their development of a campaign plan as well as the execution of that plan. These exercises are designed to present real-life challenges that a candidate or campaign manager faces in an actual campaign. The reader will need to take the information provided and analyze it with a sense of the political implications of that information. The reader will also be asked to perform some tasks that require some creative thinking. Through these exercises, the reader will find the truth in the statement that campaigning is both an art and a science.

## CHAPTER 2
## THE CAMPAIGN PLAN

### ORGANIZING A CAMPAIGN

We have noted the differences and similarities between national-level campaigns and those at the state or local level. The differences can be stark—especially when considering the amount of media attention and money spent on the highest-level campaigns. But we also identified similarities that virtually all campaigns share. For example, campaigns for state and local offices have had the opportunity to adopt some of the sophistication and knowledge that campaigns for federal office have gained over the years. One of the most important lessons learned has been an appreciation for proper planning and preparation before running for office. The product of that preparation is the campaign plan, which we believe all political campaigns should create and execute. To that end, we take the reader through the key activities that candidates and their campaigns must carry out in order to win on Election Day.

Of course, a prospective candidate must first make the decision to run for office. In Chapter 1, we told the story of Representative Collene Lamonte's particular path to office, an interesting set of circumstances that finally led to her decision to run for the Michigan state House. Of course, the decision to run should be an informed one, so that a candidate knows he or she has a realistic chance of winning.

## Organizing a Campaign

Seasoned campaigners recognize that all political campaigns have four basic resources available to them—time, information, money, and people. Because all campaigns potentially have these resources, how efficiently and effectively they are used becomes crucial. Herein lies the importance of the campaign plan. A campaign has the same amount of time as an opponent's until Election Day—how efficiently will the campaign use that time? Deciding on the best use of the candidate's time as well as that of the volunteers can make the difference between winning and losing an election.

Information can take multiple forms as it relates to political campaigns. Communicating the most effective message to voters—and being able to identify those voters—also is key. A campaign message that is repeated frequently and consistently is much more likely to be remembered by voters than a series of inconsistent messages covering a wide range of issues. In addition, a considerable amount of information about districts and their voters is available from online public records. How well a campaign organization taps into that information and uses it to identify with and mobilize voters on Election Day also can mean the difference between winning and losing.

Smart and successful candidates are able to bring together committed and skilled individuals to help with their campaign. In many cases, a state legislative campaign organization may be able to recruit only a few people who will be considered part of the core team (see Figure 2.1). Ideally, all campaigns will be able to raise and spend campaign funds in order to hire a staff and communicate to voters. But campaigns for many down-ballot offices often struggle to raise a sufficient amount of money to accomplish their goals. For example, sometimes a campaign with limited resources is only able to staff the campaign manager's position and perhaps find another person who is willing to serve as a volunteer coordinator. Whether the campaign organization has three or ten core members, a single individual will likely perform a number of different functions during a typical state legislative campaign. In short, there are many ways to organize a political campaign.

For example, some campaigns will have a core team of only two or three individuals and therefore will need to divide the many different campaign responsibilities among only a few people. Other campaigns will be able to staff the organization with an office manager, a scheduler, events coordinators, an Internet and social media coordinator, and chairs of outreach committees that

---

**Core Team Titles and Activities**

<u>Candidate</u>
Voter contact, fund-raising, speeches, events, interviews

<u>Campaign Manager</u>
Oversees all campaign activities, including field operations
Manages campaign office and staff (clerical, data input, phone calls, etc.)
Oversees maintenance of campaign Facebook and Twitter accounts

<u>Volunteer Coordinator</u>
Recruits, organizes, and helps coordinate volunteers for field operations
Coordinates GOTV and polling place volunteers

**Note:** Activities are more important than titles. If your core team has more than three members, duties can be allocated differently. In all four of our case states (CA, MI, TX, and VA), state campaign finance laws require that a candidate committee appoint a treasurer, who files campaign finance reports and is responsible for campaign finance compliance. Typically these are the treasurer's only responsibility in a campaign.

---

**Figure 2.1**   Campaign Core Team

spread the tasks around and take some of the burden off the candidate and the campaign manager. In larger campaigns, many candidates are involved directly only in fund-raising, as media spokesperson for the campaign, and in making voter contacts. The rest of the work of the campaign falls to the campaign manager and whomever else is playing a major role in the campaign organization.

## Creating a Campaign Plan

As we noted earlier, creating a campaign plan is very important to running a successful campaign. Prior planning is key to developing an overall strategy and being able to execute that strategy. In fact, in order for campaigns at all levels to have a chance of being successful, a plan of attack should be created. This plan puts down on paper every aspect of the coming campaign and how it should ideally be executed. Therefore, the best plans are in place even before a candidate files with the state to formally enter the race.

Every aspect of what will confront the candidate in the coming campaign must be anticipated and dealt with. The campaign plan allows the team to develop a strategy to win. Of course, it is quite possible that unforeseen events will occur during a political campaign. While it is difficult to plan for these surprises, campaign organizers should at least be aware that surprises might occur. These unexpected events make a campaign plan even more important, because it is all too easy to diverge from one's path to election when responding in an ad hoc fashion to problems that may arise.

In addition, all aspects of the plan should be consistent and complementary to each other, from scheduling and organizing events to making contacts with voters, and from debating the opponent to organizing GOTV efforts at the end of a campaign. As one campaign expert has noted:

> Writing a comprehensive plan forces campaign managers and strategists to think through their options. It imposes a sense of order on a process that otherwise can be chaotic and totally inefficient. A political campaign should not be merely a series of events and activities haphazardly sequenced and arbitrarily timed. It should be rolled out with clear purpose as part of a logical plan. (Faucheux 2004, 26)

Although such planning requires time and effort prior to launching the campaign, it ultimately saves time and helps avoid duplicated or wasted efforts once the campaign begins. In addition to planning for activities that are expected—fund-raisers, debates, literature drops, and so on—the plan should also help the candidate and his or her team anticipate potential roadblocks and bigger-picture occurrences. For instance, a campaign plan might include different budget figures—a high and a low budget—that accommodate the fact that a campaign may or may not be successful in raising money. If the candidate accomplishes the fund-raising goal, the campaign might operate under the high budget figure, but if the candidate is not able to meet the fund-raising goal (a real possibility for many campaigns), the campaign will be prepared to operate under the low budget figure. In other words, the plan even includes contingencies and tries to anticipate events that may occur.

A campaign plan defines what is to be done, when it should be done, who should do it, and what resources will be needed to complete the tasks (see

Beaudry and Schaeffer 1986, 43–44). A solid campaign plan lays out the contextual information of the district, voter information, campaign strategy and tactics, and staffing and resource requirements. Therefore, the major elements of a campaign plan[1] include:

- A district analysis
- Electoral research
- Candidate and opposition profiles
- The campaign message
- A communications plan, including a paid media plan and an earned media plan
- Budget and fund-raising plans
- A volunteer recruitment and use plan
- A GOTV plan
- A campaign calendar

## Detailing the Components of a Campaign Plan

In this section we add some detail to the plan components introduced in the preceding section. The next section discusses the contextual information about the district a candidate is seeking to represent. The research conducted on the district and its voters can be key to the success of a campaign because it gives the candidate a sense of what the people in the district are like and what kind of district it is generally. In some cases, this research will help a potential candidate determine whether a run for office is even feasible.

### District, Electoral, and Candidate Analyses

A district analysis provides information on the district's geography, economy, infrastructure, transportation networks, and other relevant features specific to the district in which a candidate is running. The ideal candidate also knows his or her district intimately from having spent so much time there. This candidate knows details about the district that can be used to their advantage during the campaign. For example, the candidate might know where the well-kept neighborhoods are, details about local schools (including their sports teams and mascots), where the dangerous traffic intersections are located, and so on. Candidates who do not already know these details should learn them. Early in the campaign, a candidate and a campaign staff member might conduct a "windshield survey," driving around the district identifying and noting important characteristics. The district analysis also includes a demographic analysis of the district, including voter characteristics—partisanship, race, gender, and age. Of course, candidates with a long history and deep roots in their district will not need to conduct as much research on the district.

The key to this research is doing an analysis and making sense of the data. It is not enough to collect the information; one must be able to pull out the important political information from the data collected, interpret it, put it in the right context, and analyze it so that it is useful to the campaign. Many times this research can help a campaign to form a campaign message, develop tactics for identifying supporters, and create an overall strategy for winning the election. We have already mentioned the decision-making process involved in deciding to run for office. This includes at least a basic analysis of voting data. Based on the political characteristics of the district, does the candidate have a reasonable chance of winning? This ideally involves an analysis of historical voting results from the district. This information can inform the candidate and his or her campaign team about the kind of district in which they will be campaigning. Is it a Democratic or Republican district, or is it a swing district where neither party holds a historical electoral advantage? This electoral research and analysis can also help the campaign identify more precise information vital to the campaign. A few numbers can tell a candidate a great deal. Arguably most important is an accurate prediction of voter turnout. Being able to predict how many voters will show up on Election Day allows a savvy campaigner to estimate how many votes it will take to win the election. In a two-person race, this is simply 50 percent plus one vote; this estimation gets more difficult in races where there are three or more candidates. Other information that can be very helpful includes where the high-turnout precincts are, where the candidate's base of support is located, where the opponent's base of support is located, and which precincts have high numbers of swing voters. All of these data are important because they help state house campaigns decide how to allocate scarce resources.

Research makes up a large portion of the campaign plan, and the district and demographic analyses and electoral history make up only part of that research. The plan is nearly useless unless opposition research, which seeks to compile information about the candidate's opponent(s) that can be used to one's own advantage, is conducted. This type of research, however, goes beyond the opponent. Any sound campaign will also conduct research on its own candidate so as to be ready for whatever information the opponent's team will uncover. Opposition research typically uses public sources of information (as opposed to gossip or private information) and is relevant to the campaign (Burton and Shea 2010, chap. 3). For example, if the opponent is touting his or her fiscal responsibility but has filed for personal or business bankruptcy in the past, a campaign might use this information to counter the opponent's claims of fiscal responsibility.

Opposition research can be tricky, because making information about an opponent public can backfire. Many voters consider delving into an opponent's background and using it in one's own campaign to be "negative campaigning" and generally unfair or mean-spirited. If a campaign uses information it has collected that the public deems inappropriate, it can create a backlash that can damage the candidate's chances. Not all opposition research is unseemly, however. An example of personal information relevant to a campaign is the scenario noted above where the opponent is touting his or her fiscal responsibility but has filed for personal bankruptcy in the past. The candidate's campaign might use this information to counter the opponent's claims of fiscal competency or trustworthiness. Moreover, campaigns are about providing potential voters with a choice. Pointing out differences between two candidates (and therefore creating a contrast) cannot be done without knowing what the opponent has done or said in the past and what they have promised to do in the future. Typical opposition research investigates a candidate's past political life (if they have held or run for office before) through his or her roll-call voting record and other decisions he or she has made—what policy solutions have they supported (or failed to support) in the past—and public statements about public policy and solutions to problems. The emergence of social media has created more opportunities for campaigns to conduct opposition research—and for candidates to get into trouble for postings on YouTube, Twitter, or Facebook. Just such a situation occurred in 2011 and 2012 in Troy, Michigan. Janice Daniels won a close election for mayor of Troy in November 2011. After the election, a Facebook post she had made before she was elected became public, and it was a major reason she was successfully recalled in November 2012. She had posted the following statement on Facebook after the state of New York began permitting gay marriages: "I think I am going to throw away my I Love New York carrying bag now that queers can get married there" (Abbey-Lambetz 2013). When this statement became widely reported sometime after the election, it set off a firestorm of controversy, and each one of her statements and actions after that was scrutinized and debated. Even though she made the statement before she became mayor, the story reveals how social media can be a liability for candidates.

One of the first questions people ask a candidate is "Why are you running?" This single question is the central piece to any candidacy. It is a question to which every candidate must have a clear and concise answer. Candidates will hear this question when they go door to door, in small group meetings, and during media interviews. The best example of the importance of this question is a candidate who could not answer it satisfactorily—or succinctly. During his unsuccessful 1980 bid for the Democratic Party's presidential nomination, Senator Edward Kennedy (MA) was asked in an interview why he was running for president. After several minutes of rambling on about a number of things, it was clear that Kennedy did not have a direct and simple answer for this seemingly simple question.[2]

In part because of Ted Kennedy's experience in the 1980 race, many observers and practitioners of political campaigns increased their attention to the campaign message (Vavreck 2009). A campaign message is a short statement that explains why voters should support a candidate (and not the opponent). Put another way, a campaign message emphasizes one candidate's competitive advantages over his or her opponent(s). As such, the message is the foundation of what the candidate will want to communicate to voters throughout the campaign. The most effective campaigns reinforce the same message in every speech, in every door-to-door conversation, in all campaign literature, and in all interviews and debates. Only through continual repetition will the candidate's rationale for running sink in with the electorate. In other words, the message should reverberate through every portion of the campaign and campaign plan. Because the message often provides information about candidates and issues, it is important to know enough about the district (i.e., district and demographic analyses) and each candidate (i.e., candidate and opposition research) to be able to create comparisons that will be advantageous. Remember, campaigns are about giving voters a choice, and it is the campaign's job to show voters why their candidate is the preferred choice.

Along with opponent and candidate research, some campaigns conduct a SWOT analysis (strengths, weaknesses, opportunities, threats) of the candidates, the context, and the issues. Strengths are factors that can be counted as assets by the campaign, including certain attributes of the candidate (e.g., incumbency, expertise in a certain issue area, or strong name recognition among the electorate), support from major voting blocs in the electorate (e.g., African Americans, union members, voters from one area in the district, or a large ethnic contingent in the district), and ample financial resources. Weaknesses can include nega-tive information from the candidate's public record (e.g., votes they have taken while in office, questionable business practices, or failing to pay their taxes) and an inability to raise money and attract significant support (Powell and Cowart 2003). Opportunities are factors outside of the campaign that might prove beneficial. These can include the state of the economy, prior voting trends in the electorate, the mood of the electorate, and a potential campaign issue that favors the candidate (Powell and Cowart 2003). Threats are factors external to the campaign that might be detrimental, including a weak economy if the candidate is an incumbent or an influx of independent expenditures made on behalf of the candidate. A threat can also be anything that might be used against the candidate, including a scandal involving an elected official from the same party. The presence of higher-level races can be either threats or opportunities, depending on the context of those races. Identifying positives and negatives about each candidate helps the campaign identify comparisons that may be useful to the candidate throughout the campaign.

A related device commonly used when developing a campaign message and identifying contrasts between candidates is a message box (see companion website for message box figure). Often a product of a SWOT analysis, a message box illustrates the strengths and weaknesses of each candidate. However, the mes-sage box goes a step further and helps a campaign identify contrasts that will give their candidate an advantage. In the message box, candidates try to define themselves, their opponents, and the issues in the campaign by dividing strengths and weaknesses into the four quadrants of the box. This helps the campaign identify what each candidate is likely to say during the campaign. In this way, a campaign can position itself relative to its opponents and be better able to offer voters choices that favor their candidate. In addition, the SWOT analysis and message box help a campaign identify possible weaknesses in their candidate or any of his or her issue positions, allowing them to strategically anticipate and respond to criticisms or attacks by an opponent.

What messages work the best? There is no standard message that will appeal to all voters in all districts across time. However, some general messages have been used consistently in campaigns at all levels for many years. For example, in a state house general election in a district where Republican Party support is clearly dominant (this would be clear from the electoral research conducted), sometimes the best message is simply "I'm the Republican candidate." However, in nearly all campaigns, the campaign team will find it necessary to create a message that reflects the positive qualities of a candidate and the nature of their particular district and race.

Closely related to the campaign message is the campaign theme. The *theme* is what the campaign is about, while the *message* tells potential voters why the candidate is the best choice. Some themes have been used again and again over the years. For instance, in his 1864 reelection campaign, President Abraham Lincoln said, "Don't change horses in the middle of the stream." Many modern incumbents still use a version of this "stay the course" theme. In contrast, challenger candidates often use a theme centering on change, urging potential voters to fire the incumbent. In 2008, Barack Obama embraced the theme of change on the heels of the presidency of George W. Bush amid an appetite for something new among the electorate. Obama's use of this theme in 2008 helped him defeat his GOP rival, John McCain. In 2012, however, President Obama was no longer in a position to argue for change. Running for reelection in what some had considered a "change" year, he used the campaign theme of "Forward." The intention was to acknowledge that more work needed to be done and President Obama was best suited to accomplish that. Messages stem from the theme and are usually more specific statements tied to issues in the campaign.

Before moving any further, we should note that we do not mean to suggest that a campaign message begins and ends with research into the district, the electorate, and the opponent. In reality, a campaign message begins with what the candidate wants to do once they are elected to office. After all, a campaign is about the candidate's vision for the future and his or her policy ideas, and it is likely that voters will ask the candidate this question throughout the campaign. As Ted Kennedy showed in 1980, to be successful, a candidate must have an idea of where they want to go once elected and what they want to do for their constituents. The research that is conducted helps refine those ideas and create contrasts between the candidate and the opponent, illustrating the choices voters have. Most of all, a campaign should define its candidate, and not let the opposition do so.

### Budget, Fund-Raising, and Volunteer Plans

A campaign budget is one of the most important elements of a campaign plan—and, of course, the campaign itself. As we noted in Chapter 1, campaigns at all levels continue to become more costly with every new election cycle, so much so that a successful campaign in a competitive race for a state house seat may cost $200,000 or even more than $1 million. The kind of research summarized above will help determine how much a successful campaign is likely to cost. However, a successful campaign can operate on a small budget. For purposes of this simulation, we have limited the amount of money available to each campaign so that readers are forced to make strategic choices that are typical of the majority of state legislative campaigns operating with relatively small budgets.

A campaign's budget serves the same purpose as a household budget—it identifies how much money a campaign has to work with and how much it needs in order to operate. The budget also details how much money is coming in and how much is going out. This kind of cash flow information is important because the campaign will need certain amounts of money at certain points in the campaign; for example, at various times it will need to pay for yard signs, postage for direct mail pieces, and other paid media efforts (e.g., TV or radio ads). If the campaign does not have an idea of what kind of funds it will need and when it will need them, it will be flying blind throughout the campaign.

Generally, a fund-raising plan is created along with the budget in order to detail how the campaign will raise the money needed to execute the budget. Knowing how much the campaign needs to spend (based on other strategic decisions outlined in the plan) will help determine how much the campaign needs to raise. The reverse is true as well. A realistic understanding of how much money the campaign can raise can provide a realistic idea of how much money the campaign will have available to spend. A major part of the fund-raising plan is to identify possible sources of contributions—from individuals to PACs to political party organizations. Remember that a growing number of "independent expenditure-only" committees might also become involved in advertising using their own message and theme.

Another aspect of campaign fund-raising is the campaign finance regulations that each state has enacted for its house races. States set limits on how much money an individual, group, or party may contribute to a candidate committee. These limits can change over time, so campaigns must be sure to know the legal limits. It is quite common for states to require that campaign representatives take a seminar on campaign finance regulations, including the schedule for reporting and penalties for failing to follow the regulations.

Down-ballot races often rely solely on volunteers for much of the day-to-day business of the campaign—stuffing envelopes, making phone calls, walking door to door with campaign literature, putting up yard signs, and working polling places on Election Day, to name only a few. While higher-level offices might hire individuals to perform some of these tasks, many state house campaigns must use volunteers for most of these activities. A well-organized volunteer recruit-ment and use plan can produce substantial benefits during a campaign and on Election Day. A good volunteer plan is prepared to effectively use any volunteers who might show up on a given day. In fact, some lower-level campaigns always make sure they have a volunteer coordinator on staff, because it may be the most important staff position after the candidate and campaign manager.

### Communications Plan

Should the candidate try to talk to every resident in the district? Of course not. First, we know that not all residents vote, because not all are eligible or regis-tered. Second, not every registered voter makes it to the polls on Election Day, and of those who do, not everyone votes for all down-ballot offices. In fact, it is quite likely that those who turn out on a consistent basis make up only around one-third of a district's registered voters. Finding those registered voters who will participate on Election Day is key to any campaign strategy. This is partly accomplished through the electoral research discussed above. However, beyond identifying potential supporters and what the candidate will say to them (i.e., the campaign message), the campaign must devise a strategy to communicate that message to those potential supporters.

A communications plan is a critical component of the campaign plan. After all, what good is the contrast between two candidates if the campaign message is not communicated to voters? A communications plan includes what the cam-paign will say and by what means the message will be delivered (e.g., TV, radio, newspapers, direct mail, door-to-door literature). There are two basic components of a communications plan: earned media and paid media.

While the type of paid media advertising employed will likely vary for dif-ferent types of races, having a sound paid media plan is just as important in down-ballot races as it is in federal or statewide campaigns. A paid media plan incorporates research conducted on the media outlets that cover the candidate's district to determine the best outlets for the campaign's message. One key deci-sion is which types of paid media will be used. Information about all television (network affiliate and cable) and radio stations (including audience demographic information as well as costs) is usually readily available, as is information on local newspapers (but remember that local news has been migrating away from traditional hard-copy newspapers to Internet news sources, such as local "Patch" online news outlets). Again, largely due to cost, campaigns at the state legislative level likely will not use any network-affiliate TV advertising, unless the district is in a minor media market and rates are not too high. Cable television is an option in some state legislative districts, but viewership is low in many cases. More often than not, the primary paid media approaches used in state legislative campaigns are direct mail and social media. Direct mail that targets individuals in the district offers campaigns the ability to communicate a specific message to specialized groups of potential voters, while social media communication through Facebook, Twitter, Instagram, YouTube, and other social media sites is inexpensive to transmit. Social media can be quite useful for campaigns at the state house level. Through Facebook, you can communicate messages to those who've "liked" your Facebook page, and your Twitter followers can be informed about the campaign and be mobilized to attend events or for GOTV efforts.

Earned media is any campaign story covered as a news item. It is sometimes called "free media" because the campaign does not directly pay for the coverage as it would with an advertisement. But as any campaign expert will attest, free media is far from free, since campaigns expend resources attempting to gain the attention of newspaper reporters, TV or radio stations, and other media sources in hopes that they will cover their campaign as a news story. Generally, down-ballot campaigns do not receive much earned media from newspapers, and they receive even less from television and radio stations.

Therefore, a carefully crafted earned media plan designed to increase the chances of receiving media coverage is vital to the larger campaign plan. Unless potential voters know that the candidate held a rally, made a speech, or attended a meeting with citizens, it might as well not have happened. To that end, campaigns need to have an idea of what strategies they are going to employ to try and attract media attention from local journalists. Knowing who the local political reporters are and cultivating a relationship with them can be a significant advantage to any campaign. Beyond that, a campaign must know how it is going to communicate the candidate's actions so as to make them newsworthy and attract media attention. However, we urge some caution here. A campaign team can expend a great deal of effort in an attempt to obtain favorable earned media coverage, but many news outlets simply do not cover down-ballot campaigns because there are so many races and candidates. Most media outlets face a choice between covering all candidates for all races (to be fair) and not covering any race, other than formal announcements of the election and election results. Occasionally there are factors that increase a campaign's salience to the public, and more media coverage is possible as a consequence. But at the level of state house races, salience is generally quite low and coverage may not materialize.

In many campaigns, especially those with few resources, a lot of time and effort is spent seeking earned media attention, but another word of caution is appropriate here because there is a trade-off between cost and control. Just because a campaign convinces a journalist to cover one of their events does not mean the resulting story will be favorable to the candidate. Any interview, speech, or other event covered by the media can reveal a candidate's weaknesses or be subject to interpretation or editing by the media.

For example, Katie Couric's interview of vice presidential candidate Sarah Palin during the 2008 campaign proved disastrous for the McCain-Palin ticket. Palin's unfocused, rambling responses during the interview caused her approval ratings to drop substantially and increased concern that she was not suited to be vice president—and potentially president. After the interview, CNN blogger and commentator Jack Cafferty said that if Palin being "one . . . heartbeat away from being President of the United States . . . doesn't scare the hell out of you, it should."[3] Even with the potential for earned media to backfire, any campaign with hopes of success must try to identify how they will attract positive attention from the local media.

### Get-Out-the-Vote and Campaign Calendar

Everything that a candidate and his or her campaign team have accomplished over the course of a campaign will be meaningless if the candidate's supporters do not show up at the polls on Election Day. Therefore, a GOTV plan is absolutely crucial, since it focuses on creating the most efficient and effective use of campaign resources leading up to Election Day. Typically, campaigns will have identified likely supporters through previous contacts (door to door, campaign events, social media followers) in the weeks and months prior to the election. In the days leading up to Election Day, volunteers can make another contact with known supporters to remind them to vote. Because elections for down-ballot offices tend to be low-information races, such reminders are even more important for state legislative elections. Remember also that some states (including our case states of California and Texas) have enacted election reforms that include early in-person voting so that voters may vote any number of days prior to Election Day. This will complicate a campaign's GOTV efforts.

Finally, a good campaign plan will include a campaign calendar. Earlier we emphasized the importance of time and noted the time constraints all campaigns work under, as there is an ever-decreasing number of days until Election Day. However, time is also one of the resources a campaign has at its disposal, even if it is the most scarce (candidates can always try to raise more money, but they cannot add hours to the day or extend the campaign beyond Election Day). Campaigns with hopes of winning must have a handle on what is going to happen and when it needs to happen. Of course, a candidate and his or her opponent both have the same amount of time until Election Day—no one has a built-in advantage. This makes developing a sound strategy and a campaign plan even more important, because they can give one candidate a huge advantage over the other. Many questions about the calendar must be asked. For instance, when does the candidate begin his or her door-to-door walking? When do the direct mail pieces go out? When are the fund-raisers scheduled? When can lawn signs be put up? Timing is crucial in terms of the campaign budget, as raising and spending money allows all the other activities in the campaign to go on. More importantly, a campaign needs to know at what points it will need certain amounts of cash—to send direct mail, order lawn signs, or hold another fund-raiser—and how that money is going to be made available. These and many other issues must be addressed. One method employed by veteran campaigners is to plan backward in time—starting from Election Day (remembering that some states allow early voting on multiple election days) and working back toward the candidate's announcement—to fill out the campaign calendar and form a flow chart of sorts which, when implemented correctly, can get all the parts of the campaign moving in a coordinated fashion. The campaign calendar puts all of the above components of the plan together into a useful document.

## Conclusion

When brought all together, the campaign plan is a document that can be used throughout the entire campaign. When the unexpected happens (which can be something the campaign does by mistake, something the opponent does that requires a response, or something completely outside of the race), the plan will inform the campaign as to the best approach to take. In other words, even when facing the unexpected, a good plan can help a campaign decide whether it is worth it to do something that is not part of the plan, to respond within the context of the plan, or to simply continue to follow the plan without specifically responding.

The importance of the campaign plan cannot be overstated. Without a written plan of attack, a campaign will likely not be successful. While it takes time, effort, and resources to create a campaign plan, it gives a candidate a better chance of winning on Election Day. It may seem easier to run a campaign without going through the effort of creating a plan, but the time spent preparing will result in time saved when the campaign is in full swing. It is better to take time at the beginning to develop and design a strategy to win than to be left on election night wondering what went wrong.

This chapter has provided an overview of the campaign plan and its rationale. The next chapter includes the exercises that make up the simulation. They are designed to help the reader develop and execute many of a campaign plan's components.

## CHAPTER 3
## THE CAMPAIGN SIMULATION

### DISTRICT, ELECTORAL, AND CANDIDATE RESEARCH

The next two chapters describe the activities that are at the heart of the campaign simulation. Each more fully develops the steps needed to complete the components of a campaign plan, which we introduced in Chapter 2. We have divided the core simulation activities into two chapters to highlight an important difference in some of the activities. Much of what a campaign does in the heart of the election cycle is informed by research that must be conducted in advance of any run for office. The components of the plan that fall into the category of preliminary research—the district analysis, electoral research, and candidate and opposition research—are covered in this chapter. The components of the plan that center on applying this research are then covered in Chapter 4.

Chapters 3 and 4 also contain a series of exercises that allow the reader to experience a range of decisions and activities a campaign team would face and carry out in a state house campaign. All of the exercises in this chapter and the next are typical of decisions that must be made and tasks that must be completed in any campaign. We have designed these exercises to roughly reflect the different parts of a campaign plan that a candidate or campaign manager would create before waging a campaign.

However, not all campaigns are the same. Indeed, they vary on many levels—the individuals involved, their decisions, the information available, and the districts in which they are running. In addition, the states in which these campaigns are run have different laws that will influence a campaign. States and campaigns also differ in the type and form of available information. We illustrate these points in our four case chapters that follow Chapter 4 and demonstrate that different aspects of the plan may need to be completed differently based on the available information. In addition, as we noted in Chapter 2, the plan template that we suggest is only one way to create a campaign plan. However, we have included the generally accepted components of a campaign plan, and we believe this will help readers better appreciate what kinds of decisions campaigners must make. Within any campaign there are several tasks and responsibilities for a number of different actors to undertake. Candidates and campaign team members have their distinctive responsibilities, but so do actors outside of the campaign. For instance, journalists play a large role in modern campaigning in that they report on campaigns and thus convey a good deal of information to the electorate. Therefore, along with exercises associated with the campaign plan, we include exercises in some sections meant to simulate activities performed by journalists covering a campaign. This is done to underscore the importance of the campaign–media relationship that exists during an election season. Citizens also have duties as well—gathering information so as to be informed about candidates and issues, and voting on Election Day.

We have divided the exercises into four sections: elements of the campaign plan that are related to the research behind a campaign; elements of the campaign plan related to creating and communicating the campaign's message; crisis management; and campaign ethics (the first of these is covered in this chapter, while the others are in Chapter 4). The elements of the campaign plan are those responsibilities that fall on the candidate and the campaign team as they seek to win the election.

No campaign goes as smoothly as a candidate would like. Something goes wrong in almost every campaign. For this reason, we present a series of crisis management scenarios that will require the candidate or team to make decisions about how to respond to the crisis.

Finally, since there are no universally accepted standards for running a campaign, questions of ethics often arise in campaigns. Those watching a campaign may not see these ethical questions, because they most likely arise behind the closed doors of the campaign. However, rest assured they do arise. Questions of what to do in a certain scenario when the right answer is not clear and decisions about how to handle a crucial situation likely come up in every campaign. Most of the time they present themselves as dilemmas—instances where there is no obvious right or wrong answer.

All in all, the following tasks, exercises, and scenarios present the reader with a range of decisions to be made and responsibilities that must be accounted for in a modern campaign. One reader's approach to these tasks may differ from another's. It can be very instructive to see how someone else handles the same question, data, or scenario.

There are a number of different roles that are part of any political campaign. In addition to the candidate, a typical campaign team could include a campaign manager, treasurer, volunteer coordinator, and volunteers. Some campaigns at the state house level hire professional political consultants to provide specific technical services, such as survey research, micro targeting of voters, social media and website coordination, and media production. However, in many state house campaigns, anyone with a free hand pitches in to help the cause. The campaign's volunteer coordinator might also help prepare a paid media advertisement; similarly, the campaign manager might end up doing much of the opposition and candidate research. In small campaign organizations like the ones in many state legislative races, there are no narrow job descriptions.

## Creating the Campaign Plan

Previously, we discussed the purpose of the campaign plan and its importance in operating a successful campaign. In the remainder of this chapter, we detail what goes into each component of the plan. We have divided the plan into ten different components across this chapter and the next, with the exercises associated with each section following directly.

### Campaign Plan Section 1: District and Demographic Analysis

The district analysis provides important background information on the district's geography, as well economic and demographic statistics. A full understanding of one's district will help a campaign team form the campaign message—the backbone of any successful campaign—and help the candidate speak knowledgeably about the district and its needs. The information culled from the district analysis will help form the message because it can help identify what the district's population is like as well as what issues may be important to district voters.

## Geography

The district analysis should include even the most basic information that one might take for granted. For example, what exactly are the district's boundaries? This is important because only voters living in the district are the target audience for the campaign. This seems obvious, but such research will affect how a campaign team targets its advertising. In addition, a good geographic analysis will give the savvy campaigner some important information about the district; for example, is the district rural, suburban, or urban, or is it some combination? Each type of district is very different and lends itself to different issues being defined by voters as important. In an urban district, for instance, public transportation or crime might be important issues, while in a rural district, agriculture or road construction might be at the top of the list. Moreover, geographic analysis can help a campaign decide which tactics to employ; for example, how realistic is it for the candidate or volunteers to walk the entire district door to door given the geographic nature of the area? Sources of information about a district usually are easy to identify and access. A detailed map of the district can be obtained from the state or county elections bureau, and other useful maps can often be found online. We have provided basic district maps for each of the districts included in this simulation, but more detailed maps that include major streets, waterways, and other important features can be found with a little research.

## Economy

Many counties or communities provide relatively up-to-date information on the local economy, often through their planning and economic development departments. The target audience for these reports is usually a business seeking information about a locality with the prospect of locating or relocating in that community. Typically, this economic information is fairly comprehensive and may be published as a "community profile," which is typically available online. The data available might include the most recent census information for the area, such as demographics, average household income, poverty levels, and unemployment rates. But they also can include labor market statistics (such as labor costs and availability, transportation, and hospitals and other health care data), government and public services that are available, crime rates, utilities, and local tax rates (as well as any available tax incentives). In addition, regional or metropolitan-wide research organizations may collect and report community profile data in certain areas.[1] Smart campaigners will collect as much data as they can on the communities within the district. This will allow them to create an accurate picture of the area in which the campaign will be waged. It also provides an opportunity to start assessing the issues important to the people in the district. For instance, if there are troubling economic indicators, they are likely issues that the campaign should address. If taxes are high and businesses have not been moving into the district, that is a signal as well. Certainly, high unemployment figures are a clear issue priority for any campaign.

## Demographics

Even if demographic information is available through the community profile, it is a good idea to consult the US Census Bureau website, which is an excellent source of critical information. In particular, the American Community Survey is a useful tool for state house campaigns; it provides detailed estimates on demographics in cities, towns, and counties over a multiyear period. We have included summaries for the areas in each district that is featured in this book. As noted above, the critical aspect of a district or demographic analysis is the *analysis*. Simply collecting statistics and information on the area without using them to inform the plan and decisions will provide little strategic value.

Readers will notice that we have provided different amounts of detail with respect to the information needed to complete the district analysis. This is because different types and levels of data are available in different states. The differences across states in terms of what information is available can make creating a district analysis easier or more difficult. For instance, in Texas, the Research Division at the Texas Legislative Council provides a wealth of data on each house district in Texas. In this case, much of the data needed by a campaign has already been compiled. All that is left for the campaigner to do is to update the data (if needed) and conduct an analysis to tell the campaign what they mean. On the other end of our spectrum is California, which provides much less easily used data. In this instance, campaigners must go to the census and collect the information themselves. This can be a challenge because, for example, the 60th District is so large, and instead of dealing with data about one city or small county, several different sources must be consulted to obtain a picture of the entire district. In addition, the 60th Assembly District in California does not include the entirety of a large city in the area—Riverside—so collecting district-specific data is more difficult.

The two other states in our simulation fall somewhere between these two extremes. There is some easily obtainable information in the Virginia case (not all from the state itself) but it is not all the information that one needs to create a strong district analysis. In Michigan, there is not much readily available information, but the district is smaller and involves only a few communities. Specifically, one can easily find census data for Muskegon County, but the district does not include the city of Muskegon. Campaigners will have to gather data on Muskegon County and the city of Muskegon and remove the city's figures from the county's totals. This is one way to narrow the data available into useful figures, but there are others, too. Campaigners will have to determine which information is available and most useful, then identify the best course of action to create a useful analysis.

## District and Demographic Analysis Exercises

1. Create a district analysis of your district. Pull out the most important pieces of election-relevant information and identify possible issues for the campaign to focus on. For example, what kinds of employment, housing, and population trends are seen in the district? What educational levels do the district's residents have? Who are the major employers in the district? What other kinds of organizations are prominent in the community (and might play a role in the campaign)? For example, are organizations such as Veterans of Foreign Wars, the Chamber of Commerce, or labor unions active in the district? The most important questions to consider after gathering this information are: What will these data mean for the campaign? What are the issues that might be important to the people of this district given what you know about it?

2. Conduct a demographic profile of your district's population. What are the people like who live in the district? Characteristics such as race, gender, age, ethnicity, poverty rate, and income should be included in your analysis, but you should go beyond these categories. Remember that you might have to go beyond the information provided to you or recategorize it so that it is more useful. Again, the important questions here are: How do these demographic characteristics impact your campaign strategy (who are your likely supporters, and what might be important issues in this district)? What issues might be important during a campaign given the demographic lay of the land in the district? How will the district and demographic analyses influence your campaign message?

## Campaign Plan Section 2: Electoral Research

Understanding the district in which a campaign is taking place includes understanding its voters. Note that we focus on voters rather than citizens or residents. When campaigning, all that matters on Election Day is how many votes a candidate receives. The electoral rules governing most elections in the United States simply state that the candidate with the most votes wins. Knowing about past voting statistics and trends is critical to understanding how to win an election. As with the district analysis, electoral research should be conducted and completed well before the campaign begins.

The importance of electoral research cannot be overstated. An analysis of a district's voting history might convince a candidate that winning the election is not very likely because voters have historically supported candidates of another party by overwhelming margins. This information may even impact a potential candidate's decision to run. However, if the candidate definitely has decided to run for office, research on the district's past voting patterns will help shape the campaign's strategy.

There are a great many areas where electoral research can help a campaign. In this simulation, we will focus on two. First, the research conducted will help the campaign team answer the critical question, "How many votes do we need to win?" A related and more detailed question is, "Where are the supporters likely to be within the district (that is, where are supporters and the high-turnout precincts located geographically)?" In answering these questions, a campaign will begin to focus on both a strategy (the general approach of how one will win the election) and a set of tactics (the specific steps in executing the strategy) that will become part of the campaign plan's framework. Second, electoral research will inform the campaign about what kind of district it is facing—is it a strongly Democratic district, a strongly Republican district, or is it a swing district where neither party has a historical advantage? Again, this information and a strong analysis of the data will inform the strategic direction of the campaign.

Campaigns for president of the United States and other high-level offices have resources to identify and track (through survey research) where voter support tends to be and what a candidate's favorability ratings are with voters. For instance, at the presidential level, knowing the states where the candidate (and the opponent) has strong support helps the campaign estimate the Electoral College votes it can count on (as well as those that are solidly in the opponent's column). In a governor's race, this might be on a regional, county, or city level. For instance, a candidate running for governor in Michigan would know from past voting trends and up-to-date polling that Republicans tend to do very well in the western and northern regions of the state, while Democrats do well in the southeast portion, in and near Detroit, as well as other larger cities such as Flint, Lansing, and Ann Arbor. This type of information can help with resource allocation, since a campaign should not spend much time and money in areas where either it has strong support or their opponent is very strong. Rather, campaigns should focus on areas where neither candidate has an advantage and more voters can be persuaded to vote for them. In state house races, this is why precinct-level information is key. Even state house districts that have seen close elections in the past likely contained precincts that were not competitive. Focus therefore should be on those precincts where swing voters reside.

More recently, due to the increasing sophistication of technology generally and social media in particular, campaigns with large infrastructures and the resources to match have been able to identify potential voters, supporters, and campaign contributors. For example, Barack Obama's campaign estimated that it had access to about 20 percent of the total number of votes they needed to win during the 2008 campaign through the list of 13 million e-mail addresses they collected from supporters; some experts estimated they might reach up to 70 percent of the votes needed to win in 2012 with their enhanced digital effort, in which they invested in social media and technology for staffers in the field (Green 2012). In down-ballot races such as those we are focusing on, some of the same tactics can be employed, such as gathering e-mail addresses, tracking followers on Facebook or Twitter, and leveraging technology when canvassing and knocking on doors. Tracking known supporters, knowing how many there are, and mobilizing them on Election Day can be key to victory.

Campaigners, however, often start with less sophisticated data. Voter history data from similar previous races and vote totals for party candidates in one's district can be invaluable to the campaign.

### Voter Statistics

The first step in answering the two key questions about the voting population (how many votes are needed to win, and whether the district leans Democratic or Republican) is to develop a picture of the district based on voter statistics. In campaigning, the adage "past performance is the best predictor of future performance" often holds. Looking back to how the district has voted in past election cycles (typically three or four "similar" elections; see below) is the essence of this kind of research.

The key factor of geography noted in the previous section extends here as well. Beneath the district level, there is a key geographic element in politics— the voting precinct. A voting precinct is a relatively small election district that allows for localized in-person voting. Precincts vary in size but typically have 2,000–5,000 voters. The number of precincts in our four case study state house districts ranges from twenty-three in Virginia's 94th District to 141 in California's 60th District. To establish a picture of the district's voters, a campaign needs to know both the overall election result and the result in each precinct. Identifying each precinct in the district is the first piece of this puzzle. This information is typically available from the state elections officer or a county or city clerk (in most cases, election results are reported by precinct as well as by district). An important benefit of conducting voter turnout by precinct over several previous elections is that it helps identify traditionally high-turnout precincts and low-turnout precincts. A campaign might want to focus their door-to-door activities in high-turnout precincts.

Campaigns need to keep in mind that district boundaries can change every ten years due to redistricting. This is important because, as we detail below, one may need to examine results from elections prior to the last round of redistricting to obtain the data needed. For example, precincts that are currently in a district may have been in another district in a previous election cycle. In the hypothetical situation in Figure 3.1, there is a clear change in districts after redistricting. Both districts are substantially different than before. Specifically, each lost eight precincts that were previously in the district; District 1 added precincts 51, 52, 59, 60, 61, 62, 69, and 70 and lost 33, 34, 37, 38, 43, 44, 47, and 48, while the inverse is true for District 2. To get a clear picture of how the current District 1 voted in past elections, one has to examine how the *precincts* in the district voted. This will involve going back to the old map and examining how precincts 51, 52, 59, 60, 61, 62, 69, and 70 voted while they were part of District 2. In the end, what smart campaigners are after is a picture of how the current district's voters have voted over time so that estimates can be made about the two important questions we outlined above—how many Democrats and Republicans are in the district and how many votes a candidate needs to win the election.

Another important component of electoral research is identifying the base party vote in a given precinct or district. This calculation can give a campaign an idea of how many party loyalists will support a candidate and how many will

## A. Pre-redistricting

| 1 | 2 | 3 | 4 | 5 | 6 | 7 | 8 | 9 | 10 |
|---|---|---|---|---|---|---|---|---|----|
| 11 | 12 | 13 | 14 | 15 | 16 | 17 | 18 | 19 | 20 |
| 21 | 22 | 23 | 24 | 25 | 26 | 27 | 28 | 29 | 30 |
| 31 | 32 | 33 | 34 | 35 | 36 | 37 | 38 | 39 | 40 |
| 41 | 42 | 43 | 44 | 45 | 46 | 47 | 48 | 49 | 50 |
| 51 | 52 | 53 | 54 | 55 | 56 | 57 | 58 | 59 | 60 |
| 61 | 62 | 63 | 64 | 65 | 66 | 67 | 68 | 69 | 70 |
| 71 | 72 | 73 | 74 | 75 | 76 | 77 | 78 | 79 | 80 |
| 81 | 82 | 83 | 84 | 85 | 86 | 87 | 88 | 89 | 90 |
| 91 | 92 | 93 | 94 | 95 | 96 | 97 | 98 | 99 | 100 |

District 1
District 2

## B. Post-redistricting

| 1 | 2 | 3 | 4 | 5 | 6 | 7 | 8 | 9 | 10 |
|---|---|---|---|---|---|---|---|---|----|
| 11 | 12 | 13 | 14 | 15 | 16 | 17 | 18 | 19 | 20 |
| 21 | 22 | 23 | 24 | 25 | 26 | 27 | 28 | 29 | 30 |
| 31 | 32 | 33 | 34 | 35 | 36 | 37 | 38 | 39 | 40 |
| 41 | 42 | 43 | 44 | 45 | 46 | 47 | 48 | 49 | 50 |
| 51 | 52 | 53 | 54 | 55 | 56 | 57 | 58 | 59 | 60 |
| 61 | 62 | 63 | 64 | 65 | 66 | 67 | 68 | 69 | 70 |
| 71 | 72 | 73 | 74 | 75 | 76 | 77 | 78 | 79 | 80 |
| 81 | 82 | 83 | 84 | 85 | 86 | 87 | 88 | 89 | 90 |
| 91 | 92 | 93 | 94 | 95 | 96 | 97 | 98 | 99 | 100 |

District 1
District 2

**Figure 3.1**  Precincts in Two Hypothetical Districts

support the opponent. In theory, the base party vote calculation is simple—it is the number of voters who habitually support candidates of one party over a period of time. In practice, the *lowest* percentage of votes a partisan candidate receives in a given election (especially in a low-information race; see discussion in Chapter 1) is considered to be the base party vote.

Calculating the base party vote for one candidate serves multiple purposes. First, it can tell a candidate what his or her prospects are for winning a general election. For example, if the candidate's base party vote is 43 percent of the district, the prospects for winning are very good. If the base vote is only 19 percent, winning will be an uphill battle. In addition, after completing the base party calculations for both parties, the remaining percentage of voters can be considered "swing" or "persuadable" voters. This, too, is valuable information, because it tells the campaign how many of the district's voters could be influenced by campaign strategies and by activities such as speeches, ads, and candidate appearances.

As with a district analysis, there is great variation in what data might be available (in a useful format) for campaigners to examine the electoral history of their district. In some states a wealth of information is available, while in others the task of creating a reliable image of the district's voters is more complex. In addition, some but not all states have voter registration by party. For instance, in California, those registering to vote declare themselves as Democrats, Republicans, having no party preference, or affiliated with another party that has qualified for registration purposes. In this instance, base party vote is provided by the state in the form of registration figures, so one does not need to compile precinct-level data. It does not get any simpler, as the state has already done the work. In California's 60th Assembly District, just before the 2012 election, 35.53 percent of citizens registered as Democrats, 40.94 percent registered as Republicans, 4.63 percent reported some other party affiliation, and 18.90 percent reported having no party preference. On the one hand, these data tell campaigners a great deal. If the candidate is a Democrat, they know over 35 percent of voters are likely to vote for them and that nearly 41 percent are likely to vote for the opponent. In other words, the campaign already knows the base party vote for their candidate and the opponent. The Democrat in the race knows that he or she is at a slight disadvantage compared to the Republican. On the other hand, the data are limited in that one does not know much about the voters who reported some other party affiliation—do some lean toward Democrats or Republicans, or are they likely to support a third-party candidate? In addition, those who claim no party preference may lean toward one party, they may be true independent voters, or they may simply not want their preferences known.

In states that do not provide party registration figures, the calculation of base party vote is more difficult. The campaigner will need to construct an image of the district by going back to prior elections and recording results at the precinct level to create an accurate picture of the current district over time. The results from past elections are usually obtainable from the county clerk or the state's chief election official websites. Still, across states there can be differences. In Texas, for instance, as in the case of data for the district analysis, the Texas Legislative Council provides election results for the current district for elections dating back to 2002. This is more than enough data to begin to construct an electoral history of a district. In Michigan and Virginia, the data compilation task is more difficult as one must access the precinct-level data and build an electoral history.

After a precinct list has been generated for the current district and electoral history data have been accessed, one can begin building a picture of the district's voters. The end product of the data collection is similar to what we present in Table 3.1, with election results for several different offices over several election years. The key here is to obtain a good cross-section of contests including federal-level elections (presidential, US House, and US Senate), statewide races (e.g., governor and attorney general), and down-ballot elections, including state house and state senate races. The exact type of race does not matter as much as having a good representation of the elections that have taken place in the district. A second important step is to go back through several past election cycles, as this will show recent voting trends within the district. Any identified shifts in voting patterns could be the result of several factors, including changing opinions among voters or new voters moving into the district.

For *each precinct* in the district, one must collect the voting results for each race in each year that will be examined. Use the list of precincts that are currently in the district as a starting point, keeping in mind that some precincts may have been in a different district prior to the last redistricting decision. After the results are gathered for each precinct, the next step is to simply aggregate from the precinct level to the district level. In other words, for each race in each year where data have been collected, add up the results to yield the district vote totals. Again, the result will be similar to the example provided in Table 3.1. After this table has been created, one can easily find the base party vote in the district.

To estimate the base party vote, look for the lowest percentage of votes received by party candidates in the district in the previous elections for which data have been collected (in our example, we provide the last four elections). Here, one is not interested in the type of election—it could be the presidential or the state Senate race. All that matters is finding the lowest percentage of votes received by *any* candidate of the party being researched. This percentage represents the absolute worst that a candidate of that party will do in an election, because it shows how many voters are the most loyal to a party, regardless of issues or candidate quality. Do the same for the other party's candidate and the campaign will have base party vote for both sides.

In the example we have provided in Table 3.1, there were a few poor-performing Democrats since 2006—the US House candidate in 2010 received just over 32 percent of the vote, and the state house candidate totaled just over 36 percent. However, the worst-performing Democrat was the gubernatorial candidate in 2010 at 29.9 percent. Therefore, Democrats in this district can assume that roughly 30 percent of the voters in this district will vote for their party's candidate, regardless of who the candidate is. In the same kind of examination for Republicans, we find that their worst-performing candidate was a state Senate candidate in 2010 who garnered 40.5 percent of the vote. Therefore, the base vote for Democrats and Republicans in this hypothetical district is 30 percent and 40 percent, respectively, while the remaining 30 percent of the district can be considered swing voters. This is one indication that the district leans toward the GOP. Another way to identify the base party vote is to track the percentage of vote support that a district has given to partisan but low-information contests. Good examples of this could be found in Michigan, where State Board of Education races are partisan, but voters typically know very little about the candidates other than their party affiliation.

This kind of research has an art to it in that seasoned campaigners may know something about a specific campaign or candidate that might make the numbers misleading. For instance, an individual might have been a strong candidate but had a scandal (alleged or real) hit their campaign just before the election. This may have caused many voters to support the opponent and thus skewed the base party vote calculation. Or, it may have been that a certain year was a bad year for one party because of national or statewide trends in politics and voter turnout. For instance, 2010 was a "nationalized" election after the passage of the Affordable Care Act (or Obamacare), which saw Democrats lose 63 US House seats. One might look at the results from that year and adjust them knowing that

**Table 3.1** Vote History Example for a Hypothetical State House District

|  | 2006 | 2008 | 2010 | 2012 |
|---|---|---|---|---|
| Registered voters | 64,007 | 63,989 | 64,112 | 64,004 |
| Turnout | 34,823 | 45,173 | 33,002 | 43,011 |
| Turnout percent | 54.4 | 70.6 | 51.5 | 67.2 |

| Election | 2006 Votes | Percent | 2008 Votes | Percent | 2010 Votes | Percent | 2012 Votes | Percent |
|---|---|---|---|---|---|---|---|---|
| **President** | | | | | | | | |
| Republican | | | 19,876 | 44.7 | | | 20,661 | 48.2 |
| Democrat | | | 23,941 | 53.9 | | | 21,433 | 50.0 |
| Other | | | 602 | 1.4 | | | 772 | 1.8 |
| Total | | | 44,419 | | | | 42,866 | |
| **Governor** | | | | | | | | |
| Republican | 18,466 | 56.4 | | | 22,842 | 70.1 | | |
| Democrat | 14,269 | 43.6 | | | 9,755 | 29.9 | | |
| Total | 32,735 | | | | 32,597 | | | |
| **Attorney General** | | | | | | | | |
| Republican | 17,536 | 53.4 | | | 17,241 | 52.4 | | |
| Democrat | 15,298 | 46.6 | | | 15,665 | 47.6 | | |
| Total | 32,834 | | | | 32,906 | | | |

|  | Votes | % | Votes | % | Votes | % | Votes | % |
|---|---|---|---|---|---|---|---|---|
| **US Senate** | | | | | | | | |
| Republican | 17,756 | 51.2 | | | | | 21,381 | 50.9 |
| Democrat | 16,921 | 48.8 | | | | | 20,624 | 49.1 |
| *Total* | *34,677* | | | | | | *42,005* | |
| **US House** | | | | | | | | |
| Republican | 18,943 | 59.7 | 23,616 | 54.2 | 21,739 | 67.7 | 24,489 | 59.0 |
| Democrat | 12,796 | 40.3 | 19,917 | 45.8 | 10,374 | 32.3 | 17,017 | 41.0 |
| *Total* | *31,739* | | *43,533* | | *32,113* | | *41,506* | |
| **State Senate** | | | | | | | | |
| Republican | 17,652 | 55.5 | | | 12,756 | 40.5 | | |
| Democrat | 14,170 | 44.5 | | | 18,737 | 59.5 | | |
| *Total* | *31,822* | | | | *31,493* | | | |
| **State House** | | | | | | | | |
| Republican | 20,747 | 64.2 | 24,624 | 57.7 | 20,375 | 63.9 | 20,888 | 51.1 |
| Democrat | 11,578 | 35.8 | 18,063 | 42.3 | 11,505 | 36.1 | 19,988 | 48.9 |
| *Total* | *32,325* | | *42,687* | | *31,880* | | *40,876* | |

*Note:* The number of registered voters in this district for this hypothetical election is 65,154.

they represent a depressed Democratic performance. To examine any potential intervening dynamics at a more local level, examining old news reports or talking to seasoned politicos in the district are two strategies for finding this kind of information.

Estimating how many votes a candidate needs to win is also a simple calculation in theory. In a two-person race, it is 50 percent of those who turn out on Election Day, plus one vote. The idea behind approximating the number of votes that the candidate will have to garner on Election Day is to help identify what kind of work must be done during the campaign given the partisan nature of the district uncovered by measuring base party vote. For instance, if a district has a Democratic base vote of 39 percent and a Republican base vote of 27 percent, a Democrat running in that district will know they can focus on turning out their base and attracting some voters who exhibit signs of being swing voters but may have Democratic leanings. A Republican in this district will know that they have a more difficult task. They must maximize turnout from the smaller GOP base and attract a large portion of swing voters.

The estimation of the votes needed to win is a multistep process. First, one needs to estimate turnout for the current election cycle. Again, one can look to past behavior in the district to predict future behavior. Start by going back to the turnout from at least two past elections in *the same kind of race* in which one is currently running (i.e., state house races) during *the same kind of election cycle*. This latter point is crucial. As we have noted elsewhere, turnout in presidential years is higher than in midterm years. Elections in odd years typically show even lower turnout. One must be careful to make comparisons of similar state house elections when estimating turnout. If the current campaign is taking place in a presidential election year, turnout from two years prior (a midterm election) is not necessarily the most accurate indicator of what one can expect in the coming election.

Once the past voter turnout percentages have been calculated, estimating future turnout is easy—simply take the average of the turnout percentages in the elections for the same office for which one is campaigning. This figure represents one way to estimate the turnout percentage for the next election.[2] To identify the number of votes needed to win, simply take the estimated turnout percentage, multiply it by the number of registered voters for the current election cycle (available online from the state elections bureau or county clerk), divide by 2, and add 1. This result represents 50 percent plus one vote of the estimated turnout—the lowest number of votes a candidate needs to win the race.[3] Many seasoned campaigners use this figure as a low estimate and aim for a higher vote total on Election Day—better to try for more votes than minimally necessary and have a safer margin of victory than to aim too low and achieve that vote total only to lose because the estimate was inaccurate.

Based on the hypothetical district shown in Table 3.1, the estimated number of votes needed to win is 16,453. This figure is determined by going back to the two previous similar campaigns—2006 and 2010—and looking at the number of individuals who voted in the type of race we are interested in—state house. We see that in 2006, 32,325 people cast a ballot for state house; in 2010, that number was 31,880. To calculate the voter turnout percentage in these races, simply divide the number going to the polls by the number of registered voters; in 2006 that would be 32,325 / 64,007 = 50.5 percent, and in 2010 the calculation would be 31,880 / 64,112 = 49.7 percent (see Figure 3.2). The average turnout percentage over these two cycles is (50.5 percent + 49.7 percent) / 2 = 50.1 percent. Once the turnout percentage—50.1 percent—has been estimated, one can figure the number of votes needed to win by applying that estimated turnout percent to the number of voters registered for the current election. In

---

2006 turnout
2006 turnout in the state house race: 32,325
Total registered voters in the district: 64,007
Turnout percentage for 2006: 32,325 / 64,007 = **50.5%**

2010 turnout
2010 turnout in the state house race: 31,880
Total registered voters in the district: 64,112
Turnout percentage for 2010: 31,880 / 64,112 = **49.7%**

Estimated turnout percentage for current election
(50.5% + 49.7%) / 2 = **50.1%**

Predicted voter turnout for current election
Total registered voters in district for this election: 65,154
Estimated turnout percentage: 50.1%
Estimated turnout: 50.1% x 65,154 = 32,642.1 or **32,643**

Estimated number of votes needed to win
(32,643 / 2) + 1 = **16,322.5 or 16,323**

**Figure 3.2**    Estimating Number of Votes Needed to Win (Hypothetical District)

this hypothetical district, 65,154 people are registered to vote; 50.1 percent multiplied by 65,154 = 32,642.1. In order to be safe, one always rounds these numbers up. This process yields a predicted turnout figure of 32,643, which represents the estimated number of individuals who will show up at the polls on Election Day in the current election. The number needed to win is simply 50 percent plus one vote. In this example, half of the expected turnout is 16,322 (again, always rounding up); adding one reveals the estimated number of votes needed to win: 16,323.

As we noted above, the types of voter statistics we describe here are available through the county clerk's office in most cases, or the state board of elections or secretary of state's office. With the "motor voter" registration reforms of the mid-1990s, many state elections bureau offices maintain centralized qualified voter file records, which track registered voters, their addresses, and (in states like California) whether they have registered as affiliated with a political party.

Though not a part of this simulation, there are some sources of information available to campaigns that can identify specific voters' history of participation (i.e., those individuals who regularly vote in general elections, those who tend to vote only in presidential elections, those who vote regularly in primary elections, and so forth). This service (usually offered through private vendors) can be very valuable to a campaign, especially in a primary election, where perhaps only a small percentage of the district's registered voters might vote. Knowing who the habitual voters are will help a campaign use its resources wisely and target its communications carefully. Also, knowing where each candidate's base voters are as well as where the swing voters are is central to a communications and voter contact strategy. In many state legislative races, knowing exactly which voters are supporters and which are not may only come from door-to-door canvassing or other personal contacts. However, some aggregate voter statistics can be helpful to the campaign as well. For example, which precincts tend to be high-turnout precincts? Which are low? For those interested in a more sophisticated analysis, the precinct-level data collection conducted to generate a picture of the district's voters can be used to estimate high- and low-turnout areas. Simply examine over time (again, only using similar election cycles) which precincts have the highest and lowest number of registered voters. One will likely discover that voting turnout patterns are fairly consistent—that the same precincts tend to be high turnout (or low turnout) over several elections. Ranking the precincts can help the campaign make key strategic decisions. For example, a campaign can use this information to decide where to emphasize door-to-door canvassing in hopes of identifying new supporters—this would be in areas that are high turnout (i.e., the voters are engaged) and are swing (i.e., neither party has a large base). A campaign can also determine where it might concentrate its GOTV efforts—in areas where there is high turnout and where the candidate's party has done well over the years. These data can also help a campaign decide where *not* to spend time or money—in areas where the opponent has a large base or in low-turnout areas.

## Electoral Research Exercises

1. Based on the data provided about your district, estimate the base vote for each party in your district. Use the example in Table 3.1 as a guide. What does this tell you about the district? Is the district friendly territory for candidates of your party, or is it hostile? How might this affect your strategy later in the campaign?

2. Using information on the electoral history of the district, estimate the number of votes you will need to win the election. Use the example in Figure 3.2 as a guide. Remember to account for any important contextual issues that may affect the current campaign, such as whether federal-level races (such as president of the United States) will increase turnout. Also, go back to other elections to incorporate more election results if the turnout in the races varies dramatically. The estimate of the number of voters needed to win is one way to set a total vote goal for your campaign and answers the question, "How many votes do I need to win?" What other factors should be considered and accounted for in this calculation?

### Campaign Plan Section 3: Opposition and Candidate Research

As noted earlier, the ideal campaign message is a combination of issues and candidate characteristics that provide an electoral advantage to the candidate over the opponent and is consistently communicated to voters throughout the campaign. While we will describe the basic process for creating an effective message in the next chapter, any sound message begins with research into the strengths and weaknesses of the candidate and their opponent. The best way to do this is to conduct an inventory of issue positions and personal characteristics (both good and bad) for each candidate in the race. Additional research needed for the message is contained in the district and demographic analyses—this will help identify which issues might be important during the campaign.

Opposition research is a process through which a campaign examines an opponent's public past in search of information that can be used to highlight reasons the opponent should not be elected to office. "Opposition research taps into retrospection. . . . It [attempts] to convey the perils of the opponent by pointing to past performance" (Burton and Shea 2010, 61). In addition to knowing as much as possible about the opposition, all campaigns should practice a strategic principle: Know thyself. No campaign should be unprepared for what the opposition might say about its own candidate based on something the candidate did in the past. "Perhaps the best way to be prepared for negative attacks is to know what the opposition might find" (Burton and Shea 2010, 61). Opposition and candidate research is a way for those involved in the campaign to get to know the candidates and to identify those areas where their candidate has a comparative advantage over the opponent—and vice versa.

Researching one's own candidate might seem simple at first glance. However, this activity requires a frank discussion between the campaign manager (usually) and the candidate—including any detailed descriptions of candidate weaknesses. This can be a difficult subject for team members to raise with a candidate because some of the material may be uncomfortable to discuss.

True opposition research focuses on aspects of a candidate's public record—this is limited to activities that the individual has engaged in while serving in public office, or elements of their life that could affect their ability to serve in office. There are several sound ideas for how to conduct opposition research and what kinds of information need to be collected (see Burton and Shea 2010), but here we will limit the discussion to two basic types of information that will allow a campaigner to identify strengths and weaknesses about both candidates: public and personal information. A candidate's public record can be broken down into the following categories:

- *Decisions made while in office.* If the candidate has been elected to a legislative body in the past, how did he or she vote on key issues relating to the district or issues that are of importance to the district? If the candidate has been elected to an executive position (e.g., city clerk, county executive), what decisions has he or she made that impact the constituency?

- *Public statements.* If the candidate has previously served as a public official or has run for office before, what has he or she said to the public and the press about public policy problems? How has he or she prioritized the issues faced as an elected official? Does this priority ranking match the public's? What policy alternatives has he or she developed to solve these problems? Do these fit the district and constituency? If the candidate is a first-time candidate this may be a bit difficult, but even first-time candidates may have made public statements as part of other activities. Have they spoken to local organizations like Rotary clubs, Veterans of Foreign Wars organizations, or the Chamber of Commerce and made statements about important issues or policy alternatives? Even statements made on social media outlets such as Facebook and Twitter are worth collecting.
- *Declared bankruptcy.* Has the candidate filed for personal or business bankruptcy? This may be relevant in a campaign where economic issues and fiscal responsibility are at the fore.
- *Arrests and lawsuits.* Has the candidate been found liable for any civil or criminal infractions? If so, what were the allegations and penalties? Has the candidate been a party to a lawsuit? If so, how recent are the lawsuits and what were the circumstances?
- *Residency.* How long has the candidate lived in the district? Could the candidate be considered a political opportunist or "carpetbagger" (i.e., moving into a district just to run for an open seat)? Beyond simple residency, it is often useful to inquire as to whether the candidate is an active member of civic or community organizations. Has the candidate been involved with charities in the community for a long time, or did he or she start to get involved right before announcing a run for office?
- *Voting record as a citizen.* Has the candidate voted regularly in all elections at all levels? If not, such information might be used to suggest the candidate does not take their citizenship responsibilities seriously.

Information about a candidate's *personal characteristics* are generally divided into the following categories:

- *Education.* Does the candidate have an educational background that makes them qualified to be an elected public official? Have they completed college, do they have an advanced degree, or have they taken a few classes toward a degree? In some districts, it may be useful to find out whether the candidate went to public or private school (and, if they have children, where they go to school). If a candidate is making public education a centerpiece of their campaign but attended private school and now sends their children to private school, their opponent could make this a campaign issue.

- *Occupational history and experience.* What has the candidate done prior to seeking elective office? Are there any special features that make them either more or less qualified? Do they have prior experience as an elected official or a business leader? Prior public service can be an advantage *or* a disadvantage, depending on the context. For example, it may be an advantage if voters are looking for experience. It may be a disadvantage if the candidate has done little in life besides running for office; he or she may be labeled as a "career politician," which voters rarely embrace.
- *Military background.* Did the candidate serve in the US armed forces? If so, did they distinguish themselves? Did they serve in a combat area or during a war?

Other personal characteristics that have been used in campaigns in the past, such as a candidate's religion, marital status, or sexual orientation, are considered by many to be out of bounds. It is up to each campaign to decide if characteristics such as these are appropriate for the campaign they are waging.[4]

A well-run campaign will also check to make sure everything on their opponent's (and their candidate's) résumé and all other claims are accurate and truthful. Did they actually earn their degree, or did they just take a few classes toward it? Did they actually serve in the military? If not, the candidate has a lot of explaining to do and may be in big trouble. It is always better to find these things out sooner rather than later.

Many campaigners find it useful to organize the information they gather into a SWOT analysis. As discussed in Chapter 2, strengths are campaign assets such as incumbency, strong name recognition, ample resources, and support from major voting blocs. Weaknesses can include negative information from the candidate's public record and an inability to raise money (Powell and Cowart 2003). Opportunities are factors outside of the campaign that might prove beneficial. These can include prior voting trends in the electorate, the mood of the electorate, and a potential campaign issue that favors the candidate (Powell and Cowart 2003). Threats are factors external to the campaign that might be detrimental, including a weak economy if the candidate is an incumbent or an influx of independent expenditures made on behalf of the candidate. We have provided enough campaign context and candidate profile information in each case chapter for readers to begin constructing opposition and candidate research reports as well as a SWOT analysis. However, readers should expand their research efforts by collecting more information about the district, campaign issues, and candidate characteristics through general web searches, social media sites, news articles, and/or phone calls to government agencies holding public documents that would be useful to the campaign.

## Opposition and Candidate Research Exercises

1. Before the campaign begins, you learn who your opponent will be in the primary campaign, as well as who the opponent might be in the general election. It is crucial to the campaign that you know as much as possible about the political backgrounds of these individuals as well as your own candidate. Write an opposition research report on your opponents and a separate research report on your candidate. What kinds of information will you look for? Also consider what kinds of information are inappropriate for this exercise. Begin with the Candidate Profile Worksheet found on the book's companion website. Then, expand your research to include other information that might be relevant to the district and the race in particular. Be as exhaustive as you can. At this stage, collecting more information than you may need is better than not collecting enough.

2. Based on the research you have conducted—the demographic and district analyses, the opposition and candidate research, and the electoral history analysis—what are the strengths and weaknesses of your candidate? What are the strengths and weaknesses of your opponent? Conduct a SWOT analysis for the two candidates.

## Wrap-up and Next Steps

The research tasks and related exercises contained in this chapter form the basis for creating a complete campaign plan. The research on a voting district, on that district's voters, and on the candidate and his or her opponent(s) often are the first steps taken once a candidate has decided to run for office. Of course, in some cases, a prospective candidate may conduct this research and decide *not* to run. Assuming the candidate wishes to move forward with his or her campaign, the remaining sections of the campaign plan must be crafted. Those sections are covered in Chapter 4. In most cases, further research must be undertaken in order to create a campaign budget and fund-raising plan, identify and recruit volunteers, develop an earned and paid media plan, put together a GOTV strategy, and find a way to fit all of these activities into a campaign calendar.

Ideally, all sections of a campaign plan (those contained in both Chapters 3 and 4) will be completed prior to the launch of a campaign, but the steps we have identified in this chapter often inform a candidate and campaign team about how to best proceed with the remaining portions of the campaign plan.

# CHAPTER 4
# THE CAMPAIGN SIMULATION

## APPLYING THE RESEARCH

While Chapter 3 covered the components of the campaign plan that involve district, electoral, and candidate research, this chapter centers on the pieces of the plan that utilize that research and apply it to the campaign. These are the key strategic parts of any campaign as they focus on the core argument for why one candidate should be elected over the other, how the campaign will communicate to potential voters, budgeting and fund-raising, and how the campaign will get their supporters to the polls.

The information and exercises in Chapter 3 illustrated that running a political campaign is both a science and an art. The exercises in Chapter 4 will underscore that principle as well. Crises occur all the time in campaigns, and there is often more than one way to deal with a problem, which can create a dilemma for a campaigner.[1] Moreover, there may be times when an individual campaigner's ethics are challenged by a situation. Therefore, we have included both crisis management and campaign ethics exercises in this chapter; both concepts are important to understanding what happens in a real political campaign. These kinds of decisions represent the art of campaigning, and at times they are more challenging than the science side.

## Campaign Plan Section 4: Campaign Message

As noted earlier, the campaign's message summarizes the central reason a candidate should be chosen over their opponent. It can also be thought of as the answer to the question one might hear while standing in line at the grocery store: "I see you are wearing a John Doe button. Why are you supporting him for the state house?" The answer, "I'm voting for John Doe rather than Joe Public because . . . ," is the heart of a campaign message.

There is no one best way to create a message. One tool used by many campaigners is a message box. The product of the research done on the district and the candidates is a set of information that, when taken together, creates the four quadrants of the message box (see companion website). The SWOT analysis done for each candidate can help make this even clearer. The candidate's strengths are those qualities or advantages that one would want to stress (i.e., the "what we want to say about ourselves" section), while the opponent's weaknesses go in another quadrant (the "what we want to say about them" section), and so on. Opportunities and threats are likely seen throughout the box.

Creating a message box serves multiple purposes. Some campaigners use it to organize their thoughts and simply list different items in each part of the box, while others begin to develop the actual message by writing a short statement based on the items in each quadrant of the box. The final message is then crafted by taking information from the box into account so that one ends up with a strong (but relatively brief) statement that offers a comparison between the two candidates and tells voters why they should vote for the candidate rather than his or her opponent.

Crafting a message may be the most difficult task a campaign undertakes. This is because there is no "right" answer to the question, "What is the best message for our campaign?" Message creation is another example of the art of campaigning. The message box is just one of many tools a good campaigner can use to develop a message from all the research and analysis that has been conducted. There is no one formula for creating an effective message.

Whatever process a campaign employs to create a message, the message should have certain characteristics. First, effective messages are short and memorable. A campaign message should not be more than two or three sentences, and voters must be able to easily remember the message. When asked why a person should vote for a candidate, supporters should be able to quickly provide an answer. Also, voters will respond to a message better if it resonates with them—that is, if it centers on issues important to them. In addition, a message typically is stated positively and should contain an obvious contrast with the opponent. Elections are about choices, and a message is the candidate's chance to show the choices available on the ballot. Finally, a message should be authentic—after all, there are real reasons a candidate has chosen to run. We caution against any message crafted simply because the campaign team believes it is what voters want to hear.

Some believe that anytime a candidate says something critical about his or her opponent, the candidate is engaging in negative campaigning. We do not agree. As we have just noted, elections are about choices. Demonstrating to voters what the candidate sees as the biggest and most important difference between themselves and the opponent is not only appropriate, but necessary. One caveat applies here—comparisons must be made in the appropriate areas, such as those we mentioned in the section on candidate research in Chapter 3. In addition, personal attacks not relevant to how a candidate will do his or her job as a representative should be avoided. As long as a candidate sticks to issues and relevant personal characteristics, the comparisons made in a campaign message are legitimate and useful.

## Campaign Message Exercises

1. A campaign is about communicating to the electorate why your candidate rather than the opponent should be elected to the state house. Therefore, any campaign needs to know what the candidate should say about himself or herself and what he or she should say about the opponent. Using the research and SWOT analysis your campaign has completed, construct a message box for your campaign. Include at least three items in each quadrant of the box. What are the most important and advantageous contrasts to draw between your candidate and his or her opponent?

2. Take the information from the message box and craft a message for your candidate. This can be derived in part from the issues or characteristics you have identified as your opponent's strengths and weaknesses, but do not forget to reflect on your own candidate's strengths and weaknesses. Usually the biggest challenge in creating a complete message box is anticipating what the opponent will say about your candidate in their message. Therefore, try to anticipate what your opponent will say (what is your candidate's greatest weakness that is publicly known?) and create a message that the opponent's campaign might use.

## Campaign Plan Section 5: Budgeting and Fund-Raising

Budgeting and fund-raising are separate but related activities. Creating a budget tells the campaign how much money it needs to raise and how it will be spent; all the things done in a campaign will cost money in one way or another. For instance, the print advertisements will have to be printed by a print shop, and if they are going to be mailed, postage will have to be paid; if a radio ad is created for the campaign, it will have to be produced and time will have to be purchased from the radio station(s); the volunteers who work hard for the campaign must be fed; and all the materials needed for research as well as crafting the message (e.g., computers, paper, and other office supplies) must be rented or purchased. The budget outlines how campaign money is going to be raised and spent. The fund-raising plan not only anticipates an amount that needs to be raised, but also details the specific strategies the campaign will use to raise the money.

There are several strategies and tactics for raising money in a campaign. However, the most successful is a direct solicitation by the candidate either in person (ideally) or over the telephone. In addition, solicitations can be made through the mail with a fund-raising letter sent to supporters. In some campaigns, PACs and political party organizations make direct contributions. Candidates and campaigns also hold events—dinners, coffees, receptions, house parties, and so forth. Sometimes a contribution is required for these events, while in other cases, the campaign is hoping that invited guests will pledge a contribution or make a donation on the spot. Online and social media are increasingly popular and low-cost fund-raising tools and can be used by all campaigns.

In sum, the basic sources of campaign funds are:

- *The candidate.* Candidates for state legislature often contribute (or loan) a good deal of money to their own campaign. A benefit of this is that a candidate can make unlimited contributions to their own campaign. Should the candidate have the funds available, he or she can self-fund a significant portion of their race (again, that figure will be different in nearly all campaigns).
- *Family and friends.* If a candidate cannot count on his or her closest allies for monetary support, they may as well not run. The funds raised from family and friends, like all individual contributions, are regulated by laws that differ by state. Campaigns must be sure to know what the legal source and contribution limits are for the state in which they are campaigning.

- *Other individuals.* Potential donors are everywhere (e.g., acquaintances from church, coworkers, neighbors, fellow members of a community organization). These individual contributions are regulated.
- *Political party organizations.* Parties are not typically the best source of money; they may be limited by state law or just not interested in contributing to the campaign because they want to focus on other targeted races. However, it never hurts to ask.
- *PACs.* PACs are similar to parties in that they may be limited in the amount they can contribute, or they may simply decide to stay out of the race. Campaigns should note what state laws and regulations apply to PAC contributions and reporting requirements.

## Fund-Raising Techniques

The strategies or techniques used to raise political campaign money are fairly standard as well, but they should be in step with the campaign plan, the candidate, and the campaign message.[2] They include the following.

- *Personal solicitations* are requests made directly by the candidate. This is best done in person and should probably be restricted to the candidate, not other members of the campaign team. This can be done at one-on-one meetings specifically scheduled for this purpose, during a phone call made by the candidate, or at coffees, house parties, and other events where supporters and potential contributors are present. The main point to remember about fund-raising is that people will not give to a campaign unless they are asked. When raising money in this way, a candidate should always try to make the potential donor feel needed and that their contribution will be doing something that is vital to the campaign. For this reason, the appeal should be tied to some specific campaign-related event or activity. For instance, a candidate could tell a potential donor, "I'm trying to raise $5,000 so we can put a radio spot on the air in two weeks as a final push before Election Day." An important thing to remember about this kind of fund-raising is that the candidate needs to convey a sense of urgency and purpose.

  In today's digital world, appeals posted on video-sharing websites such as YouTube are also possible. These lack the personal connection that can be made in person, but it is a way to reach many more potential donors and to do so quickly. YouTube is an attractive tool for candidates because it is relatively inexpensive; any campaign with a cell phone camera and a YouTube account can put a fund-raising appeal online. In down-ballot races, the inexpensive nature of this fund-raising approach makes it cost-effective.

- *Direct mail* is a technique that can be used for fund-raising as well as voter contact (see "Campaign Plan Section 7: Paid Media" below). Used as a fund-raising technique, direct mail is a written solicitation mailed to targeted households. Solicitations may be sent after purchasing a list of potential donors from a vendor. This list would likely include names of individuals who have given to political causes in the past. Direct mail is similar to an in-person appeal in that it must convey a sense of urgency. However, it is often difficult to obtain a significant return when appealing to potential donors with a direct mail solicitation, due to high costs and the ability of recipients to ignore the appeal. This is why many campaigns use direct mail fund-raising only with individuals who have already demonstrated support for the campaign and shown a willingness to contribute. Due to relatively high costs, direct mail used for fund-raising is being replaced by online fund-raising or appeals made through social media.

- *Ticketed events* include dinners, golf outings, receptions, and the like. These events have the potential to raise a good deal of money if a large number of tickets are sold at the right price—or they could be a bust. One needs to remember that events can cost a good deal of money to organize and put on, reducing the net revenue from the event, which is the real measure of success in fund-raising. Some candidates have even found that they lose money on these events. If the campaign is expecting 100 people at a dinner but only 70 show up, the campaign may end up in the red.

- *Social media and Internet appeals* are the latest advancement in campaign fund-raising. As we noted in Chapter 1, presidential candidates John McCain and Howard Dean led the Internet fund-raising world during their 2000 and 2004 campaigns, respectively. Online fund-raising efforts have expanded in scope and migrated to campaigns down the ballot during the last decade. More candidates employ this technique today than ever before. As we note below, nearly every candidate has a website. Smart candidates will invest what is needed to accept contributions through a secure site so anyone who visits the site and is moved to contribute can do so easily.

Campaigns for federal and statewide office have also led the way in using e-mail and social networking sites and applications like Facebook and Twitter to make fund-raising appeals. Those voters who follow a candidate on Facebook or Twitter are already very likely to be supporters. These are great audiences to whom to appeal for donations, as they are already on board with the candidate and want to see him or her win the election.

Online solicitations through tools like Facebook and Twitter offer other advantages. With these technologies it is much easer to have multiple contacts with a potential donor (versus, say, an event) and to go back to donors multiple times. The 2008 and 2012 Obama campaigns were very effective in cultivating small donors who gave under $200, many times under $50. When a donor makes a small contribution, they are more likely to give in the future. For a campaign, getting a donation, however small, solidifies their relationship with the supporter, whom they can solicit again in the future.

Using Facebook and Twitter also allows the campaign to easily follow up with donors after they have made a contribution. The same kind of emotional and urgent language that would be used in a direct mail solicitation should be used in these forums. But unlike mail, Facebook and Twitter allow the campaign to publicly thank donors and more easily provide them with an update on what the donated funds were used for. A message of thanks to the donors with a link to the new radio or TV spot that was paid for with the funds could go a long way toward receiving even more contributions.

Finally, remember that regardless of the fund-raising strategy, contribution limits established by each state's campaign finance laws must be followed. For instance, campaigns should not hold a $1,000-per-plate dinner if the legal limit on individual contributions is $750. Also, it is important to keep in mind that outside groups might become involved in any race. While a campaign cannot control or influence these outside groups, they may influence its fund-raising strategy.

There are different ways to approach this section of the plan. One way is to start with a budget to figure out how much money the campaign needs to raise. Using the budget, the campaign then creates a fund-raising plan to determine how (and when) to raise that money. This approach has the benefit of outlining a clear fund-raising goal—the number on the bottom line of the budget. There are problems with this approach, however. One is that the campaign may not know whether it can raise that amount of money if it has not developed a fund-raising plan yet. What happens if the budget sets a funding goal that is beyond the capabilities of the campaign to raise? The campaign could be in over its head if it proceeds with a budget figure that it cannot match on the fund-raising side. If obligations are made by purchasing certain services, such as airtime on radio or television, the campaign may not be able to meet its commitments. The reverse is also true: If a campaign finds that it can raise significantly more funds than the budget originally called for, that could also hurt the candidate's chances. If the candidate had the capacity to raise more money than expected, perhaps another direct mail piece could have been planned that would have reinforced the campaign message one more time.

A second option is for a campaign to start with a fund-raising plan and then decide how best to spend the money it predicts it can raise. This poses problems as well. If the campaign concludes that the candidate can raise only a small amount, that may not be enough to run an effective campaign. For instance, if a candidate is running for a US House seat as a challenger or in an open seat race and the campaign team thinks it can raise $500,000, they might as well stop right there—$500,000 is not enough to run competitively in a contested US House race. Of course, the amount that will allow a candidate to be competitive will vary for every race in every state. The point is that if a candidate cannot raise the funds needed, the campaign is already in trouble. Of course, if this determination is made early enough, the candidate could see it as a signal not to run. Another problem with this approach is that even if the campaign plans strategically to match the proposed fund-raising to a budget, the campaign may find that it needs to raise more money than originally planned. In other words, the race may end up costing more than the campaign expected at the early stages. If the fund-raising plan has been executed as originally designed, it may be that donors have already given the maximum allowed by law, in which case the campaign has few options available for more funds. Alternatively, a campaign may find that it needs to spend less than the candidate can raise. This is less of a problem than the other scenarios because the campaign can better plan for contingencies or spend extra money on mail pieces, voter contact, radio ads, or another campaign expense. Additionally, any money left over at the end of the campaign can be saved for the next election.

A third option is to plan a fund-raising strategy and budget simultaneously. This allows the campaign to adjust one side of the fund-raising/budget equation when a potential problem arises. Whichever method a campaign chooses, the process must begin with the campaign team sitting down to discuss the candidate's fund-raising interest and abilities. If the candidate is not comfortable asking for contributions or demonstrates tendencies that would make it difficult for him or her to do so, plans will have to be made to raise the funds in some other way. This can prove difficult, as the candidate is any campaign's chief fund-raiser.

## Budgeting and Fund-Raising Exercises

1. At the end of each case chapter is a budget figure that will serve as a contextual guide for the activities your campaign will engage in. In other words, we have created a fund-raising and budget target for you. This budget number is specific to the district in which you will be working. While that is your budget for the campaign, you still have to be able to raise that amount of money. Develop a fund-raising plan that outlines how that money will be raised. From what sources are you going to solicit funds? How are you going to solicit funds? Are you going to use direct mail, personal solicitations, social media, ticketed events, or a combination of these? Be sure to figure the net revenue from each fund-raising activity that you plan—remember, it takes money to raise money! Most importantly, be sure to operate within the campaign finance regulations set out in state law (these are covered in each case chapter). On our companion website, we have provided a campaign budget template; begin there and adjust for your campaign as you see fit.

2. You have just finalized the last print ad the campaign will mail out to swing voters (see "Campaign Plan Section 7: Paid Media" below). The campaign needs to pay the printer and the post office in two weeks. Write a fund-raising appeal for your campaign to send out on behalf of the candidate. Use the information in the section above as a guide. Remember the importance of conveying urgency and emotion in fund-raising appeals. What platform will you use to make the appeal? What issues will you address, or will you not discuss issues? How are you going to turn potential donors into donors? What else should you include in the appeal?

3. Take the same scenario in exercise 2 above. Record a video fund-raising appeal that the campaign might post on YouTube. How will your video appeal differ from the written appeal in exercise 2? What issues will you feature, if any? Will your opponent make an appearance? Think about how emotion and urgency will be conveyed differently in a video appeal compared to the written one above.

## Campaign Plan Section 6: Volunteer Recruitment and Use

For many state house campaigns, most activities will be accomplished using volunteers, at the direction of core campaign team members. For most of these races, there probably are no paid staff members at all. In some campaigns, there may be only one paid staffer—the campaign manager. In campaigns where only a few individuals are part of the core team, the organization might include only the candidate, campaign manager, a treasurer, and someone who assumes the role of volunteer coordinator. Any campaign that is able to recruit and retain volunteers will likely be more successful than one with few or no volunteers, especially when resources are limited. Campaign activities include walking door to door with the candidate, dropping literature door-to-door, making telephone calls (e.g., for voter contact, GOTV, or other purposes), working at campaign headquarters (e.g., working with computer lists, sending press releases, organizing fund-raisers), managing Internet and social media communications, stuffing and addressing envelopes for direct mail pieces, putting up yard signs, recruiting more volunteers, and helping organize and participating in campaign events.

As such, another key component of the overall campaign plan is a volunteer recruitment and use plan. The volunteer plan, which should be created early in the campaign, details how volunteers will be recruited and how many the campaign will need as well as specific volunteer activities and tasks, along with a calendar specifying when these activities will be performed. What are the primary sources of a campaign's volunteer base? Volunteers can come from anywhere. They can wander into the campaign office, sign up during a door-to-door walk through the district, or be recruited at a campaign event. However, campaign volunteer regulars typically belong to one of four groups:.

- *Family and friends* will likely be the core of a volunteer force since they have the closest ties to the candidate and will probably be the most involved in the campaign. As with fund-raising, if the candidate cannot count on his or her closest allies to volunteer, they probably will not see many others flocking to campaign headquarters.
- *Political party activists* are a good source of volunteers because they have likely been involved in campaigns before and have some knowledge about what needs to happen in a campaign. They are also fairly easy to find since the party headquarters in the area likely keeps a list of names of potential volunteers; whether the party will share that list is another matter. However, candidates can recruit volunteers at party events simply by networking and letting those

in attendance know that they are running. Those at a party event are "true believers" and may respond well to a candidate's request for help.

- *Issue activists* friendly to the candidate's position on specific issues are another good source of volunteers. These individuals will likely work very hard for the candidate simply because of their agreement on one issue. Potential groups to target include pro-life or pro-choice groups, gun-control activists or Second Amendment advocates, Chamber of Commerce members, veterans groups, environmentalists, and labor union members. The difficult part here is identifying the groups that might be willing to help the candidate and getting commitments from their members to join the campaign team.

- *University and high school students*, especially those who have internship or community service requirements to fulfill, are also prime targets for a volunteer recruitment drive. Many college campuses have College Republican or College Democrat groups, which are natural sources of volunteers. They may also have ideological groups—for example, pro-life or pro-choice groups—on campus that could be a good source of labor for the campaign.

Just because volunteers have been recruited does not mean they will show up when the campaign needs them most. Therefore, a comprehensive volunteer plan should lay out how to use volunteers when they do arrive at campaign headquarters (evenings and weekends are typical for volunteer hours). A campaign must be prepared to deal with any number of volunteers at any given time. A campaign might not see many volunteers for weeks at a time, then one day, twenty volunteers will show up. If there is not anything for them to do, they will likely become bored and leave (and probably never return). Important details of this part of the plan include estimating how long each activity will take (many volunteers become tired or bored after two or three hours). Many campaign organizations have a volunteer database that includes contact information for each volunteer as well as other information such as specific skills (e.g., computer software knowledge) or interests (e.g., telephone calling or walking the district). In this way, a volunteer's individual strengths can be tailored to the campaign's needs. Volunteers will also be happier about their campaign experience and be more likely to return. Campaigns are wise to try and limit the randomness of volunteer activity by planning specific days of work for a group of volunteers. This could revolve around a campaign fund-raiser, door-to-door canvassing, erecting lawn signs, or similar activities. All of the volunteer activity should go on the campaign calendar (see Section 10 below) so that everyone in the campaign knows the schedule for these activities. The volunteer plan is another area where social media can be a tremendous tool. Tools such as Facebook, Twitter, and Google+ allow a campaign to quickly contact and organize its volunteer base.

We would be remiss if we failed to mention another important feature of volunteering in a campaign. While they do not have their name on the ballot, volunteers are certainly part of the election pathway. With the help of volunteers, a candidate may be elected and bring about the change in policy for which the volunteers are hoping.

## Volunteer Recruitment and Use Exercises

1. Create a list of the most likely sources of volunteers for your campaign, and explain your rationale. For example, does your candidate have certain qualities or characteristics that would encourage young people, churchgoers, teachers, or other groups and individuals to volunteer? Be specific in your reasoning. Also address the following issues: How many volunteers do you expect to recruit? What will you have them do, and when will you have them do it? How will you ensure that they have a positive experience?

2. You are in the midst of a voter contact drive and you will be asking volunteers to go door to door to talk to potential supporters. However, you want them to be prepared and able to articulate the campaign's message at the first door they approach. Create a script for your volunteers. Make sure the script is short and understandable. It might start out with "Hello, my name is . . . and I am working for Joe Public who is running for state representative in this district." What other information should you include? Which (and how many) issues do you include? What should the volunteer say after providing information about your candidate and campaign? Will the volunteer ask the person he or she is talking with to do anything? After the volunteer leaves the home, does the campaign want any information recorded?

## Campaign Plan Section 7: Paid Media

Once a candidate has decided on his or her campaign message, the campaign needs to decide how the message will be delivered. Typically, candidates communicate to voters directly and in person, or through radio, TV, the Internet and social media, or mail. Direct voter contact comes through door-to-door canvassing, meetings with voter or homeowner groups, and small group gatherings of voters with the candidate (e.g., fund-raisers, coffees, house parties, meet-the-candidate events).

Although voters have more of an opportunity to meet personally with a state house candidate than with a candidate for Congress or president of the United States, most voters probably learn about candidates through paid or earned media. Paid media in down-ballot races can take the form of direct mail and literature pieces left on doors during literature drops (i.e., "lit drops"). Some radio and television ads may be run in highly competitive—and expensive—state house campaigns. More and more, however, down-ballot races are turning to technology that first appeared in presidential contests—the Internet and social networking applications—to help spread their message. Paid media also include lawn signs, campaign buttons, bumper stickers, and GOTV literature.

We begin this discussion with a must-have component of paid media for state house races: printed material such as residential lawn signs, larger signs for busy intersections, buttons, and other campaign collateral material. While not exciting, these are staples of down-ballot races like those for the state house. All of these tools help with name identification, which can be critical in a state house race. As voters make their way down the ballot, they typically know less and less about the candidates and may vote for a candidate simply because they recognize their name. Creating a strategically sound plan for where lawn signs and billboards will be placed is fundamental to any state house campaign. Of course, this plan starts with recognizing key parts of the district geographically (see Section 1 in Chapter 3), including high-traffic areas, streets that may get clogged at rush hour (should there be one in the district), and central areas of the district that a lot of voters visit. Lawn signs for individual homes tend to be in areas where fewer cars or pedestrians travel, but these can still be important because neighbor-to-neighbor communication is powerful in campaigns. Some people may not be convinced to vote for the candidate because of what the campaign says, but they may be convinced by a conversation they have with a friend or neighbor. The campaign should include these materials in its budget; there are many companies that specialize in campaign lawn signs, stickers, billboards, and other printed advertising like newspaper ads.

Some of the material used in campaign signs can also be used in the next segment of paid media—direct mail and other literature. Campaigns should use some of the same photos (do not forget to credit the photographers) and artwork in its mail and literature that it uses in its signage. This assists in message and brand consistency. A campaign does not want to confuse voters with different images (including pictures, font, and color scheme) in different paid media activities.

Direct mail is an attractive tool for several reasons. First, it is usually more economical than radio or television. Second, mail can be heavily targeted so that only individuals with specific characteristics receive particular messages. A blanket mailing to all households in the district will reach many of the opponent's supporters; this should be avoided, since it may serve to energize the opponent's base or encourage someone who supports the opponent to vote when they had not planned to.

In addition, with the advent of sophisticated data mining, campaigns can now purchase lists of potential voters in a district with political data such as how often a person votes in primary and general elections (and even who has signed ballot petitions) matched with what magazines that person subscribes to and what consumer product brands they prefer. The mixing of consumer data with political data is extremely valuable because it allows for much more narrow targeting—often called microtargeting—of messages. Consider an example where a campaign has determined that in order to win they must identify their base voters, senior citizens, and women between the ages of 25 and 40. Each of these groups will need to be contacted during the campaign, but should they all receive the same message? Probably not. It may be that base voters do not need to receive a message at all until just before Election Day, at which point the campaign will want to activate these habitual voters with a GOTV message. Senior citizens will likely respond to a different set of issues than women aged 25–40. Seniors will likely be concerned about Social Security and Medicare, while women aged 25–40 may be interested in the candidate's plans for education or his or her stance on abortion. The right mail strategy can target each of these groups with the message most likely to engage them. However, campaigns that employ this tactic should keep their messages consistent. Messages to different groups of voters can be different, but they cannot be inconsistent. For instance, a targeted message to seniors about protecting Social Security benefits should not be contradicted by a message to a different group that emphasizes reduced government spending.

Video distribution of campaign messages in down-ballot races is becoming more common as it becomes more affordable. Television ads can be targeted by channel, program, and time of day. In the example above where key segments of the population include base voters, seniors, and women aged 25–40, a campaign could target each segment with a TV ad based on shows or channels that group is likely to watch or during a part of the day when individuals in that group tend to watch. Advertising on TV for state house races, if done at all, is almost always done through cable TV systems for at least three reasons. First, airtime on broadcast TV is simply too expensive for state house candidates, especially in major media markets. Second, broadcast advertising can be incredibly inefficient in down-ballot races because districts for offices like state house are small compared to a media market's size. Too many people ineligible to vote for the candidate because they live outside the district would end up seeing the ad. Third, and arguably most important, using cable systems can allow campaigns to target certain voters based on geography. If a candidate knows from doing the precinct analysis that particular areas are high base or high turnout, he or she may want to put some advertising on the cable systems that specifically service those areas. Cable systems are often geographically consistent with cities and towns. A campaign would be wise to have information on all of the cable systems in the district's viewing area. Knowing the advertising rates is also essential. TV station sales representatives can inform the campaign about their audience's demographics, which can help with targeting campaign messages.

Another option for sending video messages is through the Internet and social media outlets. As we have noted, websites are a must for just about every candidate. Adding video to these sites is a fairly simple task, or videos may be posted on YouTube and linked to the candidate's website. Online videos are not constrained in the same way TV spots are in that campaigns do not have to adhere to 15-, 30-, or 60-second blocks of time to make a statement. Online videos can be any length, but they should not be too long. Whenever a campaign has a new video to show people, word can be spread through Facebook, Twitter, or some other social networking tool. This can drive traffic to a candidate's web page and potentially increase contributions, assuming the candidate has equipped the site with the tools necessary to receive contributions.

Online and televised messages differ in another respect. The individuals who see online video messages are likely very different from TV viewers, so the focus of the message should differ as well. With television ads, the message is going to be seen by everyone watching that particular program at that particular time. This will include voters and nonvoters alike, as well as supporters of both candidates and those who have not made up their mind. As we noted earlier, those who follow the campaign on Twitter, have "friended" it on Facebook, or regularly visit the candidate's web page are already very likely to be supporters. Therefore, the message does not have to persuade people to vote for the candidate. In contrast, televised messages are designed to persuade viewers to vote for the candidate (or not vote for the opponent). While the audience for online videos will be smaller, they are better avenues for messages asking people to volunteer, make a donation, or get out and vote on Election Day.

## Paid Media Exercises

1. Create two direct mail pieces for your campaign. To help with the look of a typical direct mail piece, locate a recent or current example from a campaign in your area. Feel free to use your own creativity to create an eye-catching piece that connects and resonates with voters. The two pieces should target two different segments of the electorate.

2. Create a video ad for your campaign. Who is the target audience? How does it differ from the mail pieces you created? [For these first two exercises, remember to focus on your campaign message and the information you created as part of your SWOT analysis and the development of the message box. Share the literature pieces and video with others, and be prepared to answer questions from reporters regarding their fairness and accuracy.]

*Press Exercise Related to Paid Media Exercises 1 and 2*

2a. As a journalist, you have just seen the mail pieces and television ad prepared by the campaign. Write a critique of the ads for your online newspaper column or blog. Did the advertisements contain relevant information? Did they contain attacks? Did they use truthful information? This exercise is called an "ad watch." For more information about these kinds of stories, conduct an Internet search for ad watches and look for news stories from television networks or newspapers.

3. Construct a campaign website for the candidate. Include all the necessary information about the candidate, how to contact the campaign, how to volunteer, and how to make a contribution. What issues will you feature? What images will you use? How can you best present your candidate to someone who visits the site?

4. Sometimes a campaign needs to move a large number of voters in their direction at the end of a campaign. This could be for several reasons—perhaps the campaign's message has not resonated with voters thus far, the voters have not been paying attention to the campaign, or the opponent has simply waged a good campaign. Relying on the research the campaign has conducted and the message that has been crafted, create another advertisement featuring the candidate that will come out one week before Election Day. This can be another video message, a print ad for a newspaper, or a radio spot that will play on the local stations. Remember this is an ad that is designed to come out near the end of the campaign. Given the late timing of the ad, will you use different types of information? Will you focus on different issues? Be creative. In addition, explain why you chose the medium you did.

### Campaign Plan Section 8: Earned Media

Earned media includes any aspect of the campaign covered as a news story. This could be a short story on the evening news about a campaign event, but it could also be any interviews, speeches, and debates that are covered by the media. Online commentary and reporting through blogs also qualifies as earned media. In addition, campaigns may send regular press releases to news outlets regarding campaign events like town hall meetings and fund-raisers. As we noted in Chapter 1, attracting press coverage in state house campaigns can be very difficult. At the very least, the local media might report on the campaign when the candidate first announces his or her candidacy, when summarizing all of the candidates running for office, and when reporting election results. Campaigns need to be ready when the press does show an interest in the candidate.

As part of an earned media plan, a campaign should identify all the ways in which it can attract coverage of the candidate by the local media. This can include press releases, media events, candidate forums and debates, interviews with a reporter, and sending the press a preview of the latest online video or other campaign communication. The candidate might also consider writing an op-ed piece for the local paper's editorial page.

As part of this work, a campaign organization should have information about all of the media outlets serving the district. Remember, there will likely be some news organizations that are located outside the district but that serve residents who live in the district. The names of reporters and editors and their contact information should be obtained before the campaign begins.

## Earned Media Exercises

1. You are part of the team working with the candidate to kick off the campaign with a bang. The candidate wants to hold a rally after he or she files paperwork with the state that makes their candidacy official. Write a campaign announcement speech for the candidate that will be given in person and also shared on social media. What should the candidate say to the electorate? What issues will be important to talk about in this speech? Remember, these are the first words that some potential voters will hear from your candidate. What might the candidate talk about so as to garner media attention?

   *Press Exercise Related to Earned Media Exercise 1*

   1a. Both candidates have announced their candidacies through speeches in the community. Write a news story covering the speeches. What did the candidates say that was important for the district? What did they fail to say? What was the reaction from potential voters who may have been at one of the speeches?

2. Write a press release in conjunction with the announcement speech that will attract media attention for your candidate. Knowing how difficult it is to get the press to pay attention to down-ballot campaigns, what should you say about the candidate? What kind of material and language should you use to attract media attention? Remember, unless the press covers it and people read or hear about it, the event might as well not happen.

3. Your candidate has agreed to debate the opponent before the upcoming election. Your team is tasked with preparing the candidate for the debate. Using the research you have done, prepare a briefing for the candidate. Be sure to include questions that you think will be posed by both the moderator and the opponent during the debate. Work with the candidate to prepare answers to these questions. Finally, try to anticipate what the opponent will say in response to questions so the candidate can have rebuttal responses ready.

*Press Exercise Related to Earned Media Exercise 3*

3a.  The candidates have just held a spirited debate about the main issues
in the campaign. Write a news story that reports on the debate and
how the candidates handled themselves. Did they talk about issues?
Which ones? Were they issues that are important to the district?
(Note: To be a good reporter in this exercise, you must know a good
deal about the district. Therefore, performing your own district and
demographic analyses will be beneficial.) Did the candidates attack
each other? Did they answer the questions sufficiently? Did each
candidate ask the other candidate good questions?

## Campaign Plan Section 9: Get-Out-the-Vote

In the week or so before Election Day, a campaign puts most of its energy toward
GOTV efforts. By this time, the campaign will have identified likely supporters—and the campaign will want to make sure these supporters vote! GOTV
efforts should also be organized around absentee voting, which usually begins
at least one month prior to the election when absentee ballots are sent to voters.
Local election officials determine exactly when this happens.

GOTV activities can take a number of forms. Reminder telephone calls to
identified supporters can be made the evening before Election Day. As noted
above, social media is an important tool for campaign organization. There may
be no better example than GOTV efforts. A campaign that has built a strong
database of supporters and their contact information can inexpensively reach these
individuals on Election Day. This communication may be written and transmitted
by text or e-mail, or a link to a video can be shared in a similar fashion. Another
tactic is to have known supporters of the candidate send "friend-to-friend" messages as a reminder to vote—and to support the candidate—through Facebook
and Twitter.

Ideally, the campaign will be able to send volunteers to each of the district's
polling locations to hand out literature throughout the day. However, if the
campaign cannot cover all of the precincts for the entire day, polling places
should be prioritized so that the high-turnout polling places are covered during
high-volume times (before work, lunch hour, and after work). A GOTV strategy
also needs to be mindful of where the candidate will be throughout Election
Day. Usually the candidate votes early, then visits high-turnout polling places.

Of course, the campaign's strategy will place the candidate at strategic polling places during peak voting times.

## Get-Out-the-Vote Exercises

1. As Election Day draws near, you are in the final push for votes. The election is going to be close, and every vote will be crucial. Devise a GOTV plan for the final weekend before Election Day. This should include a detailed plan for what the candidate will do, including where he or she will spend time and activities in which he or she will engage. In addition, include a full list of tactics the campaign will employ to turn out as many supporters as possible, using the information above as a guide and starting point. Also include a list of specific activities and duties for volunteers during this last weekend.

2. Create a GOTV video that will be shown on the campaign website. What will the message be? Will this message be different from the ones you created in the Paid Media section? How can you increase the chances that those who see it will do what you want them to?

## Campaign Plan Section 10: The Campaign Calendar

All general election campaigns work within the same time constraints (for example, the amount of time between the primary and general elections). Proper planning helps ensure that time-consuming activities can be completed before Election Day. Specific dates for certain activities (e.g., when lawn signs go up and when mailings go out) must also be identified. To accomplish this, a campaign creates a campaign calendar, usually working backward from Election Day. The campaign calendar specifies the dates by which all campaign activities need to be performed. In addition, the timing of fund-raisers must correlate to when funds must be spent. In other words, the calendar is interwoven throughout the entire campaign plan, since timing plays a key role in all activities. For instance, if the campaign knows it will send out a mail piece on September 15, it must have the requisite funds before the piece is scheduled to be printed and sent to the post office. In addition, the candidate will not be able to finish walking door to door in the important precincts within the district if the time required to do so has been miscalculated or the needed number of hours have not been accounted for on the calendar. The timing of volunteer activities, including the purchase of related materials (e.g., literature, yard signs, flyers), must all be coordinated. Fund-raising events must be planned weeks in advance to allow time to secure a facility, plan a menu, book a caterer, and sell tickets. An organized campaign always has an advantage over a campaign that has not planned its calendar.

Campaigns must keep in mind that the candidate may have other obligations that must be met—these also should be placed on the calendar. For instance, many candidates for down-ballot races keep their regular job while running for office. A candidate's work commitments must be recognized and accounted for all the way through Election Day. The candidate may also have family obligations. All of these activities need to be placed on the calendar so everyone knows what needs to happen and when.

## Campaign Calendar Exercise

1. Being in the right places during a campaign is important. Certain events that happen in the district throughout the course of the campaign are "musts" for the candidate to attend (many of these are community events and can be discovered by consulting the local Chamber of Commerce or board of tourism). Create a calendar of events for the month preceding Election Day. What kinds of activities should your candidate be engaged in? How do you balance the other responsibilities of your candidate (e.g., work, family) with those of the campaign? Also, keep in mind dates such as when it is legally permitted for lawn signs to go up and when campaign finance reports have to be filed. Fill in the calendar with as much detail as possible.

The detailed information about the ten components of a campaign plan presented here and in Chapter 3 have prepared you to tackle the case studies in Chapters 5–8. Completing the exercises that accompany each piece of the plan will set you on your way toward crafting a plan that could be used in an actual race in each of the districts covered in the case studies. As we noted earlier, the case chapters and the companion website provide enough information for you to begin work on the exercises, but they are incomplete by design. To maximize what you get out of the exercises, you will have to supplement the information in the chapters and on the website with your own research, glean the important information from that research, and apply it to the context of a campaign.

## Additional Exercises: Crisis Management and Campaign Ethics[3]

In real-life campaigns, crises and ethical dilemmas can arise, often unexpectedly. In many cases, campaigns must respond and react in a short period of time, especially since social media can spread a story widely within hours or even minutes. Oftentimes the campaign's response must come in the form of a public statement to the media.

### Crisis Management[4]

The exercises presented below may be introduced at various points during the campaign simulation, or they may be considered by themselves. They are designed to stimulate thinking about situations in which different and sometimes competing interests must be handled. The exercises simulate the kinds of challenges that most campaigns will face. In real-life situations, a candidate or campaign spokesperson must respond quickly in an attempt to fix a problem. The scenarios described below will test a campaign team's organizational, public relations, and crisis management skills.

- State election law requires that all campaign material and mailings include a disclaimer disclosing the name of the campaign committee that paid for the literature (e.g., "Paid for by the Committee to Elect Jane Doe"). A direct mail piece that you ordered in a quantity of 10,000 comes back from the printer with no disclaimer on it. You are scheduled to mail it in two days, but your volunteers are arriving in six hours to stuff it into envelopes and prepare it for mailing. What do you do? Explain your decision.
- In the campaign you are running on a shoestring budget, you have asked your nephew to be your social media coordinator, since he is a whiz with Facebook and Twitter. He is talented but inexperienced in politics. After seeing a video on the opponent's website, he is angered that someone could say negative things about you. He sends three unauthorized tweets from the campaign's Twitter account and posts unauthorized messages on Facebook that attack members of the opponent's family. However, he did not tell you about this. Since sending the original tweets, he has deleted them, but they

have been seen and retweeted by many. Now a reporter is calling you to ask about the negative campaigning in which you are engaged. What do you say to the reporter? What do you say to your nephew?

- Your candidate comes into campaign headquarters very angry after hearing an opponent's attack ad on the radio. The information in the ad is documented, but it is misleading and taken out of context. How do you handle the immediate problem with your candidate? Do you recommend responding to the ad? If so, how and why? Explain.

- A local reporter claims to have discovered information that reveals your candidate smoked marijuana "on at least several occasions" while in college ten years ago. Your candidate cannot be reached. As campaign manager, you receive a call from a reporter who asks for an immediate response. The reporter's deadline is one hour away. You sense the reporter is writing a very negative article. How do you handle the phone call? What do you do in the next hour? Would your strategy change if the drug involved were different?

- At your campaign's town hall meeting with voters, your candidate has made some off-the-cuff remarks about the opponent's position on abortion that could be construed as offensive. You notice that in the back of the room is a person you know has volunteered for the opponent in the past. He has a video camera with him and looks to be in a hurry to leave the event. What do you do?

- A husband and wife each have made a $250 contribution to your candidate's campaign. This morning, they call campaign headquarters. They have heard what they consider to be a negative ad on the radio that your campaign put out recently against your opponent. They feel they cannot support you any longer because they do not like the tone or approach of the campaign. They are seeking to have their contributions returned to them. What do you do? Explain why.

- After an early-morning breakfast meeting, you walk into your campaign headquarters at 10 a.m. on Monday and are given the following phone messages:

  a. The most-watched local TV news station called for your candidate's reaction to a public opinion poll they commissioned that has your opponent leading your candidate 50 percent to 35 percent, with 15 percent undecided. They will air the story on the noon news program and on the evening news.

  b. Your lawn sign captain called in to say that most of your campaign signs in Precincts 1, 2, and 7 have been taken down or moved to unauthorized houses. Many residents have called campaign headquarters, and some have contacted the media, to complain.

c. Your volunteer coordinator has been trying to reach you. There are ten unhappy volunteers waiting in the office, ready to mutiny because they are tired of dropping literature every day. You were planning to have them drop literature again beginning at 10:30 a.m.

How do you prioritize your time between 10 a.m. and noon in responding to issues raised in parts a, b, and c? Explain.

## Campaign Ethics[5]

The following exercises present a series of ethical dilemmas in which the best course of action is not immediately obvious. When thinking about these dilemmas, consider the different facets of each scenario as well as the actors and issues involved. You should consider not only who is involved, but also how the situation affects the campaign you are involved in, both short-term and long-term.

- You are sitting in a restaurant when you realize that the people in the booth behind you are staffers from your opponent's campaign. You overhear them discussing important strategic information about their campaign. Specifically, they are discussing the content for their next direct mail piece, which is to go out next week. The piece will be very critical of your candidate on the issue of education, a centerpiece of your campaign agenda and message. Do you use this information in your own strategic planning? Why or why not?
- You are having a drink in a bar when you see your candidate's 19-year-old daughter enter, show an ID, and order a beer. When she sees you, she laughs and says, "Remember, you never saw me here." Not only is she underage, but her parents also disapprove of drinking on religious grounds and are very strict. What do you do?
- A member of your candidate's "kitchen cabinet" hands you an envelope containing $4,000 in cash and explains that a group of the candidate's friends, who wish to remain anonymous (but who also have already contributed the maximum amount allowed by state law), took up a collection of $500 each and would like to contribute it to the campaign. What should you do?
- As the campaign manager, you are concerned about your candidate's performance in a crucial upcoming debate. Returning from lunch, you find the list of debate questions on your desk. A note signed "A friend" suggests that you drill your candidate on these questions. Do you use this information? If so, do you tell the candidate how you obtained it?

- Your opponent is campaigning as an experienced businessman. Research into the public record has revealed that several years ago he ran into financial trouble in another state after overextending his credit on his home mortgage and a loan on a recreational vehicle. As a result he lost his home, two cars, and a boat. Should you use this information? Is the answer different if your opponent has been using the issue of fiscal responsibility as a centerpiece of his campaign?
- A college student who supports your candidate has offered to pose as a volunteer for the opponent's campaign in order to get inside information. She has never been to your campaign headquarters and is not connected with the campaign, so you can easily deny knowing anything about it if she is caught. Do you accept her offer?
- You have discovered in your candidate research that your own candidate has an inaccuracy on his résumé that gives a false impression of his military service (he claims to have been promoted to captain, but he never received the promotion). It will probably not be noticed, so can you just ignore it? Is your answer different if your opponent falsely claims to have been awarded a Purple Heart? Why or why not?

## Wrap-up and Next Steps

This chapter concludes the heart of the simulation. You are now ready to dive into the case studies and work toward creating a campaign plan for candidates who might run in these districts. Keep in mind, however, that crises and unexpected events are likely to occur in actual campaigns. The crisis management exercises above will help prepare you to handle whatever situations might arise during a campaign. In addition, be sure to think about ethical issues that might come up as you work through the case studies or are out on the campaign trail. It is one thing to win; it is another to win ethically.

## CHAPTER 5
# TEXAS HOUSE DISTRICT 144

As the second largest state in the nation in both land mass and population, Texas commands a great deal of attention in modern American politics. Texas is the home state of former presidents Lyndon B. Johnson, George H. W. Bush, and George W. Bush; only four other states can claim more presidents as their favorite sons. After the 2010 census, the state added a whopping four new congressional districts to its total; after reapportionment, the state held thirty-six seats in the US House. After the 2012 elections, twenty-four members of the Texas delegation were Republicans and twelve were Democrats. Republicans running in 2012 US House races received over 57 percent of the vote, the same percentage Mitt Romney garnered in the presidential election. Since 1980, a majority of Texans have voted for the Republican presidential candidate. It took another southerner, Democrat Jimmy Carter, to beat the GOP candidate, Gerald Ford, in the 1976 election. Some presidential contests have been close, but since 2000 no GOP candidate for president has received less than 56 percent of the vote. In 2012, Barack Obama won a majority of the vote in only 26 of Texas' 254 counties.

Texas has provided a number of other newsworthy political events, including Governor Rick Perry's run for president in the 2012 GOP primaries, which ended following a mistake he made in an early debate.[1] In 2013, state Senator Wendy Davis gained national attention when she took to the floor of the chamber to filibuster a bill that would have strengthened abortion restrictions in the state; she turned this notoriety into a run for governor in 2014. US Senator Ted Cruz became a media sensation almost immediately after his first election in 2012.

Many Americans know the Texas state motto—"Don't Mess with Texas"—but few realize that its original meaning was not a directive to leave the state alone, but rather an environmental message put out by the state Department of Transportation to promote less litter on Texas highways.

## Texas's Political Context

Much of contemporary Texas politics is informed by the state's economy, culture, diverse population, and rich history. While the economy in Texas is diversified and varied today, in the past it was based on producing, processing, and shipping goods to external markets. For much of its history, "the Texas economy was dependent on external demand and the prices paid for three products: cotton, cattle, and petroleum" (Haag, Keith, and Pebbles 2003, 33). For instance, "King Cotton" was grown across Texas and barged down Texas rivers to the Gulf of Mexico, where it was shipped throughout the United States and Europe. Cotton was the "economic heart" of Texas during its early years as a state (Keith et al. 2012, 24). Even today, Texas produces more cotton than any other state in the United States.

Cattle is another commodity that has been, and continues to be, important to the economy of Texas. Early on, the cattle business consisted of rounding up stray cattle found across the state. By the late nineteenth century, however, Texas had taken advantage of a growing demand for beef and turned it into an economic boom. In the early 1900s, the largest ranch in the state, XIT, had so much land devoted to cattle that it was using over 1,500 miles of fencing (Keith et al. 2012).

Cotton and cattle have remained important to the Texas economy. Today, the average cotton harvest yields roughly 5 million bales of lint and 2 million tons of cottonseed, and Texas remains the number one cattle state with about 11 million head. Even so, the biggest economic impact comes from the petroleum and petrochemical industry. "For much of the twentieth century, petroleum was the basis for the Texas economy. From the first major oil discovery in 1901 at Spindletop, near Beaumont, . . . Texas and the production of crude oil have been synonymous" (Keith et al. 2012, 25). While the United States looked for less expensive oil elsewhere in the world, the 1970s oil embargo put in place by the Organization of Petroleum Exporting Countries (OPEC) led to an economic expansion in the state. This was followed by a downturn in the oil markets in the late 1980s.

The modern Texas economy is more diverse, global, and tech-heavy and includes biotech corporations, computer software and hardware companies, and aerospace industries, among many others. Texas had a gross state product (GSP) of nearly $1.4 trillion in 2013.[2] This puts Texas at thirteenth in the world among nations, behind Australia and in front of Spain.[3] The most economically diverse areas of Texas are the urban areas, such as the Dallas-Fort Worth metroplex, but even those areas most dependent on the historic economic drivers have altered and diversified their economies (Keith et al. 2012).

Texas is divided into nine regions that have different cultural, economic, and political tendencies—Panhandle (which includes Amarillo), West (Lubbock, Midland, and San Angelo), North (Dallas and Fort Worth), East (Tyler and Lufkin), Central (Austin), Gulf Coast (Port Arthur and Corpus Christi), South (Laredo and Brownsville), Southwest (El Paso), and German Hill Country. (See Maxwell, Crain, and Santos 2014 for a detailed description of these regions.) While regional definitions are useful, it should be noted that "cultural divisions are often blurred and transitional," meaning there is not always a large divide between the regions. For example, the state's largest city, Houston, is located at the intersection of the East, Central, and Gulf Coast regions (Maxwell, Crain, and Santos 2014, 8).

Why are there so many regions in Texas? In part it is because Texas is so vast—nearly 270,000 square miles—and because so many different races and ethnicities have contributed to Texas's makeup. These groups include Native Americans, Hispanics, African Americans, Anglos (defined as non-Hispanic whites), and Asian Americans. Today, Texas is one of the most diverse states in the United States. Indeed, it is one of four states—Hawaii, New Mexico, and California are the others—whose population is majority-minority, or where the majority of the population is from underrepresented minority groups. According to 2012 US Census Bureau estimates, the Texas population is about 44 percent non-Hispanic white, 38 percent Hispanic, 12 percent African American, and 4 percent Asian.

As noted above, Texas has voted for the Republican presidential candidate since 1980. After the 2012 elections, both US senators from Texas were Republicans, and Republicans held a strong advantage in the state's congressional delegation, with twenty-four members to the Democrats' twelve. In 2014, the vast majority of statewide elective officials—including governor, lieutenant governor, attorney general, and various commissioners and judges—were Republicans. In the state legislature, Republicans also had majority control, holding 95 of 150 seats in the State House and 19 of 31 in the State Senate during 2014. The Texas legislature is considered part time; the Texas Constitution limits the meeting of the legislature to 140 days every two years (see Table 5.1). The governor, however, can call the legislature into special session, which has happened more often in recent years (Maxwell, Crain, and Santos 2014). This creates a true citizen legislator model in Texas, since members of the legislature receive only limited compensation for their service and have a career outside of government.

While Republicans dominate the state's elective offices, the citizens of Texas do demonstrate some variability in both party identification and ideology. In a recent survey of registered voters in Texas, 46 percent reported that they considered themselves Republicans, while 44 percent said they thought of themselves as Democrats. At the same time, more respondents said they considered themselves "conservative" (45 percent) than said "liberal" (21 percent), while the rest, 34 percent, said they thought of themselves as "moderate" (Ramsey 2013). Another dynamic in Texas is the Tea Party. While this anti-government, anti-tax movement did not begin in Texas, it does have strong roots there. Indeed, one of the most popular public figures among Tea Party faithful is US Senator Ted Cruz, and many other Republican members of the Texas congressional delegation are sympathetic to the group's goals. Residents of Texas are also supportive

**Table 5.1**   Texas at a Glance

| | |
|---|---|
| 2012 state population (est.) | 26,060,796 |
| 2012 number of US congressional seats | 36 |
| Number of state senate seats | 31 |
| Number of state house seats | 150 |
| 2011 state senate district population (target) | 811,147 |
| 2011 state house district population (target) | 167,637 |
| 2010 House District 144 population | 161,859 |
| Voter registration by party | No |
| Full-time legislature | No |
| Legislative term limits | No |
| Independent redistricting commission | No |

of the Tea Party. In a survey at the end of 2013, 19 percent of respondents said they would vote for a Tea Party candidate and 22 percent said they would vote for a GOP candidate.[4]

The conservative tendencies of many Texans should not come as a surprise. Much of what drives Texas's political culture is linked to modern conservative principles. Indeed, "the ideological context for Texas politics and government centers on a Texan Creed. The Texan Creed incorporates many of the same ideas that were influential for other Americans: individualism, liberty, constitutionalism, democracy, and equality. . . . Among the five ideas, individualism holds a special place for most Texans" (Keith et al. 2012, 13).

Election Day in Texas tends to see lower voter turnout compared to the United States generally. Indeed, Texas usually ranks near the bottom in turnout among the fifty states. In the 2012 and 2008 presidential elections, Texans voted at a rate that was double digits lower than the national rate. The 1988 election was the only time turnout in Texas came within 5 percent of the national figure, yet the state still ranked forty-sixth in turnout. Similar patterns emerge in midterm election years; turnout has been more than 10 percent lower than the nation in three of the last four midterms and has not ranked higher than 42nd since 1990.[5]

There are few legal restrictions related to voting in Texas.[6] Those who have been declared by a judge to be mentally incompetent may not vote, nor can those convicted of a felony who have not completed their sentence (i.e., currently incarcerated or on parole, supervision, or probation). In 2012, the total population of felons who could not vote was nearly 475,000.[7] Texans must register to vote before casting a ballot in either a primary, general, or special election; anyone wishing to register must do so 30 days prior to an election. Because of Texas's large Hispanic population, registration materials are available in Spanish as well as English.

Two other aspects of casting a ballot in Texas deserve mention, as they can impact a campaign plan. First, in 1987 Texas adopted early in-person voting. Between seventeen and four days before Election Day, Texans can cast a ballot in person at a variety of locations, including grocery stores, churches, and schools. This can have a big impact on a campaign's GOTV efforts. The reform's impact on turnout has been small, however. Also, there is not a relaxed absentee ballot law in Texas. The few groups that may vote by mail via absentee ballot include those who plan to be away from their precinct, those who are sick or disabled, and those who are over 65 years of age.

A more controversial change in Texas is the adoption of a voter identification law, which requires anyone wishing to cast a ballot to show an approved form of state identification. If someone wishes to cast a ballot but has no acceptable identification, they may cast a provisional ballot, which also allows someone to cast a ballot if their name does not appear on the voting rolls. An individual who has identification, and whose name does not exactly match but is "significantly similar" to how it appears on official voter rolls, may sign an affidavit and then cast a ballot. This law, and others like it across the United States, has a clear division of proponents and opponents. Proponents, typically Republicans, argue that it helps control voter fraud. Opponents argue that it dampens turnout, especially among groups who tend to vote Democratic—African Americans, the poor, and young people. The first year the law was in effect was 2013. "Officials said that statewide, 2,354 provisional ballots were cast this election, which is about 0.2 percent of voters. In the last off-year election, in 2011, there were 738, or 0.1 percent of the ballots cast that year" (Lyman 2013). The impact this law has on voter turnout will be monitored by many in the coming election years, both in Texas and across the nation.

Some states have very strict campaign finance laws, including low limits on contributions to candidates, while others have much looser campaign finance laws. Texas falls into the latter category. As Keith et al. (2012) note, much of what exists in Texas campaign finance law has come about as a reaction to scandal. Candidates in Texas were not required to disclose their contributions and expenditures until 1973, and even then only candidates who faced opposition had to do so. In 1991 the state Ethics Commission was created and now serves as the entity that receives state campaign finance reports. Candidates for many offices in Texas are required to file their reports electronically. There are no limits on how much individuals or PACs can give to candidates for office, except in the case of judges.

As with voter registration materials, the Election Day ballot is printed in Spanish in many counties in Texas. Since the passage of the Voting Rights Act in 1965 and amendments to the Act in 1992, the US Justice Department has required "political subdivisions"—these tend to be counties—to print ballots in a language other than English whenever a single-language minority group reaches 5 percent of the voting age population or 10,000 in number. After the 2010 Census, Harris County, which includes Houston, was required to print ballots in Vietnamese in addition to English and Spanish.

## Characteristics of the 144th District

There are 150 seats in the Texas State House. It is one of the largest lower chambers in state legislatures across the nation; Connecticut, Georgia, Missouri, New Hampshire, and Pennsylvania are states that have larger lower chambers. The target number of residents for each district in the State House after the last round of redistricting was 167,637. The total 2010 population in the 144th District was 161,859 (about 3.5 percent less than the target population); the voting age population of the district was 108,509.

Only after a long and protracted redistricting battle were the characteristics of the new 144th District known. The plan originally passed by the legislature created a district that was more heavily Republican than the district that had been in effect until 2010, as was the case with several other districts due to the GOP's control of the redistricting process in Texas in 2012 (Ramsey and Murphy 2011). In fact, in the originally designed new 144th District, statewide Republicans would have beat statewide Democrats by an average of 26 points in 2008 and 2010. The district also contained fewer Hispanic voters than it did previously. As noted in the lawsuit challenging the legislature's original maps, the originally proposed 144th District would have been significantly less Hispanic than the district that was in effect previously.[8] A federal district court threw out the original plan and imposed an interim plan for the Texas House, but it was ultimately vacated by the US Supreme Court. The Supreme Court ordered the district court to create another plan. In this map, the new 144th District was labeled a "Hispanic opportunity district" by the district court.[9] This was due in part to the fact that the minority population in Harris County increased by over 700,000 while the Anglo population decreased by 82,000; at the time of the district court's revision, Hispanics made up 23 percent of the voting age population in Harris County.[10]

The entire 144th is located in Harris County, which includes Houston and many of its suburbs. As noted above, this is an area of Texas that has seen tremendous growth in its Hispanic population. In fact, the 144th's population is 70 percent Hispanic (Batheja 2012). The district stretches from the city of Houston, a small portion of which is included within the district borders, across Upper San Jacinto Bay and Duck Bay into Baytown. It also includes parts of South Houston in the southwestern corner of the district, Pasadena, and Deer Park. The district includes a sizable industrial area along the northern tier of the district north of the Pasadena Freeway. This part of the district "is in the heart of the region's blue-collar petrochemical/refinery area" (Houston Chronicle 2012). The Houston Shipping Channel is a major border for much of the district in the north, except where the district extends across the channel toward Cloverleaf. A large park honoring the Battle of San Jacinto, the decisive battle in Texas's war with Mexico in 1836, is also in the district.

Even though the 144th is in an area that might signal strong Democratic leanings, the politics of this district exhibit many tendencies of a swing district. The district voted for John McCain over Barack Obama in 2008 by about 3 percent, but it supported Obama by about 2 percent over Mitt Romney in 2012. The district voted for Democrat Bill White over Rick Perry in the 2010 governor's race by nearly 8 points. However, in what might be used as a proxy for party identification given the lack of party registration figures, the district on average supported the Democratic candidate for the Texas Supreme Court over the Republican candidate by nearly 10 points in 2008 but supported the GOP candidate over the Democrat by nearly 4 points in 2010 (Haenschen 2012). In 2012, the 144th was an open-seat contest; the previous office holder, Republican Ken Legler, had passed away unexpectedly in June 2012. However, he had already decided not to run, at least in part because of the district's newly drawn lines. At the time of his decision, Legler noted: "Those that know me know I do not back down from a fight. . . . I seem to always enter a contest as the underdog and exit the victor. I have no reason to believe that 2012 would be any different. However, the sad fact is that the Federal Court has seen fit to give me a district that will be a constant electoral struggle every two years throughout the decade. That is a political distraction from legislative responsibilities that I choose not to accept" (Holley 2012). The fact that two campaign newcomers were competing in the general election made this toss-up district all the more competitive. It ended up being the closest race in Harris County.

## The Candidates

### Mary Ann Perez (D)

Mary Ann Perez has lived in the area that makes up the 144th district for a long time. She went to Milby High School, which is now just outside the district borders. Perez earned a business administration degree from the University of

Houston-Downtown, one of four institutions in the University of Houston system. After college, Perez began building an insurance business; today she owns the Perez Insurance Agency, which is located just outside the district borders. She built a reputation of community involvement during her time as president of her neighborhood civic association and in her service on the board of directors of her sons' Little League program (Houston Chronicle 2012). At the time of the election, Perez was 50 years old, which is about average for state legislators in the United States. Perez is a member of the Mexican American Legislative Caucus, the UH Downtown Alumni organization, and the Greater Houston Partnership, among other organizations.

In 2009, Perez was elected to the Houston Community College (HCC) board of trustees and served as chair until her resignation in 2013 before taking office in the state legislature. During her time on the board, she worked to improve the facilities at HCC. She voted to add a $425 million bond proposal to the 2012 ballot in Houston that would raise the property tax in order to contribute to updating technology at HCC and expanding the campus (Batheja 2012). In addition, she fought to reverse steep state budget cuts to education, including a $64 million cut to HCC in 2011.

### David Pineda (R)

David Pineda is a highly-decorated former US Marine who served between 2002 and 2008 in Afghanistan, Bulgaria, and Oman. At the time of the election, he was 28 years old. He was also completing his college studies at the University of St. Thomas. At the same time he was serving as a substitute teacher in the Pasadena public schools; he attended Pasadena schools as a child. He is a member of Afghanistan Veterans of America, Iraq Veterans of America, and the Lone Star Veterans Association.

During the 2012 campaign, Pineda focused on traditional Republican issues such as taxes and the budget; he proclaimed himself as a candidate with a "pro-business mindset" (Batheja 2012). Pineda was an active campaigner, knocking on over 28,000 doors in the 144th District over the course of his campaign (Jennings 2012). He also enlisted the support of some high-powered Republicans in Texas, including Tea Party darling and US Senator Ted Cruz. While his lack of experience was seen by some as a negative, Pineda touted it as a benefit, saying, "I don't have all the baggage that comes from, say, being involved in the bureaucratic system for so long. . . . I don't come with those bad habits" (Batheja

2012). Pineda said his honesty and willingness to serve were more important than his lack of experience.

## Web Resources to Help Create a Campaign Plan

The discussion of the context surrounding Texas's 144th State House District and the candidates who ran in the 2012 context provides the reader with enough information to begin conducting district and demographic analyses as well as candidate profiles for the simulation and the exercises in Chapters 3 and 4. However, we have not included all of the information that exists on this district or the candidates who competed against each other in 2012. While we have provided the reader with some fundamental information about the state, the district, and the candidates, there is more information to discover. In order to complete the exercises in Chapters 3 and 4, you may use the information we have provided in the chapter, the supplemental information on the book's companion website, and additional information that you may find. For instance, there is more information available online, such as reporting on what the candidates said and did during the election of 2012, that will be helpful when planning a future race. There is also more information about the district. Of course, finding this information is only part of the work; the real key to crafting a quality campaign plan is to analyze the information collected so it helps achieve victory on Election Day.

As you work through the different case chapters, it will become clear that the amount of information available can be quite different across states and state house districts. This occurs on at least two levels. First, as we have noted earlier, attracting media coverage of these campaigns can be difficult. In some districts, the news outlets barely cover the campaigns at all, while in others the media provide a good deal of coverage. On another level, some states simply provide more information than others about elections, the population, and other factors that will be important to a campaign. Texas is a fine example of a state that provides a wealth of data and information. For instance, the state of Texas provides detailed demographic information about each state house district, including information on the age, race and ethnicity, occupation, income level, and other important characteristics of the district's population. Other states do not provide this level of detail and campaigners must find it themselves. Texas also provides several years' worth of election results. This is incredibly valuable information that will help a campaign answer important questions. You will see as you work through the different case chapters just how different states are in terms of providing district-specific information.

For this and the following case chapters, we have provided supplemental material on the book's companion website. Remember that the resources provided to you offer specific data that were available for the 2012 election cycle, but not beyond. Therefore, when conducting the simulation for elections after 2012, be sure you obtain updated information to complete your analysis of the district, candidates, issues, and even budgets. There are, however, some baseline pieces of information we have provided for each chapter. These fundamental pieces of information include:

- *A map of the district.* The map included shows the general location of the district within the state. This map will help you familiarize yourself with the district and the lay of the land where the campaign will be waged. It will also show you where the district is situated in relation to other communities in the area. A more detailed map of the district can tell you what kind of district in which you will be working—urban, rural, suburban, or a combination. That kind of map can also help with some aspects of campaign strategy such as whether the candidate will go door to door or whether canvassing of this kind is out of the question because of the district's geographic elements. Also included are links to information on recent redistricting decisions in Texas, which have been controversial and faced several legal challenges. This will help you create a district analysis.

- *US census data on the 144th Texas State House District.* As we noted above, the state of Texas provides a great deal of information about the demographics of the 144th District; this is provided on the companion website. The information provided is specific to the 144th District and will help you create a district analysis. It is wise, however, to gather more information. For instance, you might want to examine the specific demographic patterns in the different communities that make up the 144th.

- *News articles on the campaign.* We provide links to online news accounts of the candidates and their campaigns. These will help you create a candidate and opposition research report for this campaign as well as a message box. Again, there is more out there for you to find about the candidates. Use what has been provided as a starting point.

- *District voting data.* Information on the electoral history of the district may be the best example of the voluminous amount of data provided by the state of Texas. In most states, campaigners must cobble together election results from prior years in order to determine in what direction a district leans. This is not the case in Texas, where the state provides detailed election results for six election cycles. These data will help you create a voter analysis, which you will use to determine the number of votes you will need to win the election, calculate base party voting figures, and create a targeting strategy for the district.

- *Campaign finance information.* We have provided actual 2012 campaign finance reports from the two candidates, as well as a link to the National Institute on Money in State Politics. These show who the campaigns got their money from and what they spent it on. While we have tried to keep this simulation as realistic as possible, we deviate a bit from the real world here. The race in 2012 for the Texas 144th State House District is competitive; therefore, more money likely would be spent in this race than in a state house race that was not competitive. More money means more things can be done and a wider variety of tactics can be utilized. However, we do not make it that easy for you! We took a realistic budget figure and discounted it slightly. This lower figure will force you to make some tough choices when completing some of the exercises. Just about anyone can run a campaign that is flush with cash. The real challenge comes from having to divvy up scarce resources in an efficient manner. The budget you have to work with in the race for Texas's 144th State House District is $300,000. This will help you prepare a campaign budget (including spending decisions for communications, voter contact, and paid media) and a fund-raising plan. It also will help in preparing a campaign calendar.

## Wrap-up and Next Steps

The material in this chapter will provide you with much of the information and data that you will use for your campaign simulation. While we have provided background information and useful links to public information about laws, election results, and district location, the exercises outlined in Chapters 3 and 4 provide more specific instructions about how to proceed in putting together a campaign plan. We have also provided a table on the book's companion website called "Steps in Creating a Campaign Plan," which briefly summarizes the steps you should take when preparing a plan. In addition, we have left some information for you to find on your own—much as you would need to do if you were participating in an actual campaign. Good luck!

## Chapter 6
# Michigan House District 91

The state of Michigan is known for its two distinctive peninsulas, including the lower one that looks like a mitten. The area that became Michigan was a center of French fur trading in the eighteenth century, then became a major center for timber production in the nineteenth century. The state's Upper Peninsula was a center for timber production in the 1800s but later became a source for iron ore and copper as the United States industrialized. The state is surrounded by four of the five Great Lakes: Michigan, Superior, Huron, and Erie. As a water transportation center, Michigan grew in population and economic importance, especially after the completion of the Erie Canal in the 1820s. Many people from New England and New York state moved to Michigan during this period. The names of some of the suburbs north of Detroit—Troy, Rochester, and Utica— reflect this migration pattern from upstate New York.

The state's economy in the twentieth century centered on automobile production. The state, and the metropolitan Detroit area in particular, grew at a spectacular rate along with the auto industry. Jobs were plentiful, and Michigan remained an important manufacturing center throughout the first half of the twentieth century. In addition to Detroit, cities such as Pontiac, Flint, and Lansing grew as locations for automobile production facilities and their suppliers. Cities outside of southeast Michigan grew as well, with both Grand Rapids (known for furniture making) and Battle Creek (breakfast cereal) growing in population and economic importance during this time. Other areas of Michigan, especially in the northern half of the Lower Peninsula, continued to consist of largely small towns and rural areas whose economies depended mostly on agriculture. The dairy industry is important in Michigan, and the state is also a major producer of apples, blueberries, sugar beets, and cherries.[1] In addition, Michigan depends on tourism, hunting, fishing, and recreation, given that it has many inland lakes and is surrounded by four Great Lakes.

Michigan's 2013 population was estimated at 9,895,622.[2] The state currently has fourteen congressional districts and therefore has sixteen electors that vote in the Electoral College during presidential elections. Since the US Supreme Court first mandated reapportionment in the 1960s[3], Michigan has lost several congressional seats (and Electoral College votes) due to its relative population loss since the 1970s. As such, Michigan's congressional delegation declined from nineteen in the 1960s to fourteen after the 2010 Census.

Michiganders who ran for president include George Romney, who ran in the 1968 Republican primary, and Mitt Romney, who was born in Detroit. Michigan voters supported Democratic presidential candidates in each election between 1992 and 2012. In the 2012 presidential election, Barack Obama took Michigan's Electoral College votes with 54 percent of the state's popular vote, outpacing his overall 51–47 percent popular victory nationwide. Michigan also was home to former President Gerald Ford—the only unelected president in US history.

## Michigan's Political Context

During the twentieth century, Michigan grew to become the eighth largest state in the country, thanks to the rise of the auto industry and the migration of many people from the rural American South looking for work. Many sought jobs in the automobile and defense industries during World War II; during the postwar boom they sought a chance at the American Dream. By the latter half of the twentieth century, about half of the state's population of 10 million was located in the southeast region, which includes the cities of Detroit, Ann Arbor, Monroe, and Port Huron. While Detroit and its inner-ring suburbs have been largely Democratic, wealthier areas farther out of the central city have trended Republican in past elections. In addition, the largely rural and small-town areas of western and northern Michigan have tended to support Republican candidates, at least since the 1970s. For example, Michigan's second congressional district (where our case state house district is located) is considered to be the most Republican district in the state. Among the representatives elected from this area over the years are Republicans Marvin Esch, Carl Pursell, Peter Hoekstra, and Bill Huizenga. This congressional district also has supported Republican presidential candidates in each election since 1992, giving Mitt Romney a substantial (56–43 percent) edge in 2012, even though Romney lost the state to Barack Obama.

The Republican Party, which claims Jackson, Michigan, as its 1854 "birthplace," dominated Michigan politics prior to the 1930s. The Great Depression, however, gave Democrats an opportunity to wrest control of state government from the Republican Party. Control has switched back and forth regularly ever since. Michigan has been closely divided, reflected in the tendency of Michigan voters to choose a governor from the party opposite the one holding the US presidency. This two-party competitiveness has existed for much of the post–World War II period, except for a more conservative shift that began in the 1980s and produced a large number of "Reagan Democrats" who supported President Reagan in both 1980 and 1984. Indeed, as of 2014, Michigan Republicans held the governor's office, had majorities in both the state senate and state house, and had a majority of seats on the state's supreme court. Even though the state's supreme court justices run on a nonpartisan ballot in the general election, they are nominated by parties, and parties spend a considerable amount of money sponsoring advertisements for their candidates (Klemanski 2013).

While Michigan has tended to vote Democratic in presidential years, off-year elections have been much kinder to Republicans. Republican have dominated the state senate since 1982, and the state house has been Republican for fourteen of the last sixteen years. After the 2012 elections, both US senators from Michigan were Democrats, but the US House delegation had a 9–5 Republican advantage.

The decline in manufacturing employment and union membership has reduced the clout of the United Auto Workers (UAW), but public-sector unions including the Michigan Education Association (MEA) started growing in the 1960s. The MEA has been successful organizing educators and has been a conduit for both contributions to candidates and the recruitment of teachers to become candidates for the Michigan legislature. However, education reforms—including charter schools—and right-to-work laws have reduced the size of the MEA and its influence in recent elections.

For state house candidates, access to the ballot is relatively easy. A partisan candidate may either submit 200 signatures (600 for an independent) or pay a

$100 fee. This is much easier than the congressional requirement of 1,000 signatures (which does not have a fee option). Consequently, a third-party or independent candidate can easily run for office and may have a decisive impact on a close race. Michigan voters adopted term limits in 1992 through voter initiative to the state constitution. These limits are among the shortest in the nation, with a lifetime ban on legislators after six years in the House and eight years in the Senate (see Table 6.1). Michigan thus allows House members to serve up to three two-year terms and Senate members to serve up to two four-year terms.

Consequently, the Michigan legislature has moved away from a professional model where legislators spend years in apprenticeship en route to a long career of public service in the state legislature. Term limits have resulted in significant and frequent turnover in the state house. Although incumbency is still an advantage, long-entrenched incumbency is no longer possible.

Due in part to the competitiveness of the state's politics, voter turnout in Michigan is relatively high compared to other states. As a percentage of the voting age population, voter turnout in Michigan was 64.7 percent in the 2004 presidential election, 66.2 percent in 2008, and 63 percent in 2012.[4] Over the past twenty years, many states have adopted election reforms seeking to increase

**Table 6.1**   Michigan at a Glance

| | |
|---|---|
| 2012 state population (est.) | 9,882,519 |
| 2012 number of US congressional seats | 14 |
| Number of state senate seats | 38 |
| Number of state house seats | 110 |
| 2011 state senate district population (target) | 260,000 |
| 2011 state house district population (target) | 90,000 |
| 2010 House District 91 population | 90,126 |
| Voter registration by party | No |
| Full-time legislature | Yes |
| Legislative term limits | Yes |
| Independent redistricting commission | No |

voter participation. These reforms have included early in-person voting, no-excuse absentee voting, and Election Day registration. Michigan had not adopted any of these reforms as of 2014. However, it was the first state to allow voters to register (or update their voter registration information) while they renew their driver's license at a Secretary of State office. Michigan adopted this reform in 1975, about twenty years before the National Voter Registration Act ("Motor Voter") required states to expand voter registration opportunities for their citizens.[5] In addition, the state does not require voter registration by party, which means primary elections are considered to be open. This makes it more difficult for political campaigns to identify potential supporters. Although Michigan does not allow no-excuse absentee voting, the state's graying demographics mean that increasing percentages of voters cast absentee ballots in the month before Election Day. Campaigns must shift their GOTV efforts earlier in the calendar because absentee votes are mailed out a month before Election Day.

Michigan requires strict accounting of campaign spending with detailed campaign finance reports for its legislative candidates, with all contributions requiring itemization. These reports are posted on the Secretary of State's website, so the activities of the candidate committees are easily accessible. In 2014, Michigan doubled the limits imposed on direct contributions made to candidate committees. For example, individual contributions to a state house race are limited to $1,000 (up from $500) for each election (i.e., primary and general elections as well as special elections).

Political parties have a $10,000 contribution limit, but party caucus PACs are not limited and can be significant players in close races. In 2012, the House Republican Campaign Committee spent $2.4 million, and their counterparts on the Democratic side anted up $1.8 million for a handful of races. Because of the state's interpretation of the *Citizens United* decision, spending on candidate-focused issue ads goes unreported. Because of the more relaxed campaign spending rules since 2010, most outside money is not under the direct control of the candidate.

## Characteristics of the 91st District

Michigan's state legislature is comprised of thirty-eight state senate districts and 110 state house districts. After the 2010 census, the target population of a state senate district was 260,000 and the target population of a state house district was 90,000. In 2011, the 91st State House District was drawn to encompass a population of 90,216—very close to the target. The size of this district means that grassroots campaigning is possible in terms of time and effort required as well as money.

There are thirty-four precincts in the 91st District. The district has been considered fairly competitive over the past few elections (both before and after the 2011 redistricting process), and the 2012 election was no exception. Some observers have noted that turnout can be a major factor in who wins in this district (Alexander 2012b). As with many US elections, voter turnout in Michigan increases in presidential elections then decreases in midterm elections, especially among voters who tend to support Democratic Party candidates.

The 91st District is located in west central Michigan and surrounds the city of Muskegon, but it does not include the city. As such, the district is largely rural, with small towns and townships in the "out-county" (i.e., not including the dominant city of Muskegon) areas of Muskegon County. These communities include the townships of Blue Lake, Casnovia, Cedar Creek, Dalton, Egelston, Fruitport, Holton, Montague, Moorland, Ravenna, Sullivan, and White River, along with the cities of Montague, Norton Shores, Roosevelt Park, and White-hall. Most of these communities are near Lake Michigan's shoreline, and both Norton Shores and White River Township have shorelines on Lake Michigan. The 91st State House District boundaries were modestly changed after the 2010 census (two townships were removed), so after the 2011 redistricting decision the district remained largely the same as it was in 2010.

The area's economy is primarily agricultural, along with some tourism that is related to Lake Michigan and the several inland lakes in the area. The major road through the district is US Highway 31, which travels north to south through Muskegon County. Interstate 96 (which has its eastern terminus in Detroit near the Ambassador Bridge to Canada) reaches its farthest western point as it interchanges with US 31 near Norton Shores and the city of Muskegon. While it is located outside of the 91st District, there is a deep-water port in the city of Muskegon that is important to the district's economy. The port transports goods as well as ferry passengers to and from Milwaukee, Wisconsin.

Among the district's major manufacturing employers are Alcoa-Howmet Castings, Dana Corporation, Eagle Alloy, Wesco Oil, and MasterTag. The 91st District also is home to the Blue Lake Fine Arts Camp (located in Twin

Lake) and a portion of the expansive Manistee National Forest. The Lakes Mall, a regional shopping center, is located in the district in Fruitport Township.

## The Candidates

### Holly Hughes (R)[6]

Holly Hughes, aged 56 in 2012, is a former Republican National Committee-woman who first ran for the legislature in 2008 against Democratic incumbent Mary Valentine. Hughes lost that race but returned in 2010 to capture Michigan's 91st District seat. Timing helped, as 2010 was a good Republican year, since many voters had anxiety about Obamacare. Hughes served as a White River Township trustee and was on the Montague Area Public School Board before running for the legislature. A Republican Party activist, she served in a variety of positions in the county party and congressional district organization, including treasurer, county chair, and district chair. She has continued to serve on a number of boards, including for hospitals, parks, and recycling, along with the West Shore Symphony Orchestra.

As a freshman legislator, Hughes sponsored bills to increase the income tax deduction and extend Renaissance Zones, which allow for commercial redevelopment. She also bucked her party numerous times, on issues such as education and environmental policy.

In her first term, Hughes served on the Health Policy, Local Government, Military and Veterans Affairs, and Natural Resources committees. Hughes earned a reputation as a moderate, with a 65 percent conservative voting record, the second most moderate among Republican House members. She is pro-life and stresses her experience as a businesswoman who can increase jobs, preserve the environment, improve education, and expand affordable health care, all while lowering taxes.

As the incumbent in 2012, Hughes was endorsed by a wide variety of interest groups, including Right to Life, the National Rifle Association, Citizens for Traditional Values, the Small Business Association of Michigan, the Michigan Townships Association, the Chamber of Commerce, the National Association of Manufacturers, and the *Muskegon Chronicle*. Hughes is married with two children. She has lived in the district her entire life and worked in two family businesses: MasterTag, which makes horticultural labels, and Bolema Lumber, a hardware store. She also claims extensive experience in property management.

### Collene Lamonte (D)[7]

Collene Lamonte, aged 45 in 2012, is a high school math and science teacher in Muskegon Public Schools who is in her first race for public office of any kind. She previously taught middle school in the Anchor Bay (MI) School District. Collene attended Adrian College and Oakland University, then earned a bachelor's degree from Saginaw Valley State University. In 2007 she and her husband Jeff moved to the Muskegon area, where Jeff got a job with an aluminum company and Collene began teaching in Muskegon. Collene lives in Montague, a small town located on White Lake and the White River, not far from the White Lake Channel that empties into Lake Michigan. She and her husband have two children. As a public school teacher, Collene made education, especially school funding, a top priority in the 2012 election.

In her 2012 campaign literature, Lamonte expressed opposition to corporate handouts and business tax breaks. She opposed taxes on senior citizens as well as cuts to education spending. As part of her campaign, she hosted a campaign website and a Facebook page. In 2012, Lamonte received endorsements from the Michigan Professional Firefighters, the Michigan Education Association, the Sierra Club, Clean Water Action, the County Road Association of Michigan, and the Michigan Retailers Association.

### Nick Sundquist (L)

Libertarian Nick Sundquist, aged forty-seven in 2012, is an Air Force veteran who owns an auto body repair shop and lives in Norton Shores. He ran for the Michigan Senate in 2010 in the 34th District. The Libertarian Party recruited him to run for that seat and raise the party's profile. Sundquist supports a voucher system for public education, with the hope that the public system would cease to exist after it was supplanted by a completely private system. He also wishes to abolish all tax incentives, the Michigan Department of Environmental Quality, and the state's Occupational Health and Safety Administration (replacing it with insurance company inspectors). As a Libertarian, he would also support the legalization of drugs and prostitution. He believes in getting government out of people's lives to the greatest extent possible. Sundquist, a

Roman Catholic, is pro-life. In 2012, he provided voters a unique alternative to the Republican and Democratic party candidates. Sundquist is married with three children.

The presence of a third-party candidate can complicate a campaign plan and strategy. The third-party candidate must be assessed to see how much support he or she will receive and which major party candidate will be the most negatively affected. In a close election (which was predicted for 2012), a third-party candidate who takes even 2–5 percent of the vote total can change the outcome. Sundquist received 4.6 percent of the vote in 2012. There were reports that supporters of Holly Hughes and some elections experts felt that Sundquist drew enough votes away from Hughes to give the election to Lamonte (Alexander 2012a).

## Web Resources to Help Create a Campaign Plan

The discussion of the context surrounding the candidates for the Michigan 91st State House District campaign provides the reader with enough information to begin conducting district and demographic analyses as well as candidate profiles for the simulation and the exercises in Chapters 3 and 4. We have provided the following information on the book's companion website that you will use when completing the exercises in Chapters 3 and 4. You may also want to conduct an Internet search for district, census, and voter data on your own.

- *A map of the district.* The map included shows the general boundaries of the district you will be researching. A detailed map of this district will show you quickly that this is a rural district, located near the area's largest city, Muskegon, but not including a major city within its borders. This kind of information can help your campaign determine some aspects of your campaign strategy, such as whether the candidate and/or campaign volunteers should go door to door or whether you should focus on other ways to contact voters. This map will help you when you compile your district analysis.
- *US census data on the 91st Michigan House District.* This information will be the beginning of your research into the district and the voters of the district that you will use in several of the exercises in Chapters 3 and 4. On the book's companion website we provide census pages for Muskegon County and the city of Muskegon. For your district analysis, you will need to take out the data for the city of Muskegon, since it is not in the 91st District. In addition,

there may be other pertinent data on the district that will help you complete the exercises. This information will help you create your district analysis.

- *News articles on the campaign.* We provide links to news accounts (from the *Muskegon Chronicle* and mlive, an online news source) that preview the race and describe the candidates and their campaigns. These will be useful in several of the exercises. However, you may wish to visit other websites (of the candidates, of other news media, or of "good government" organizations). This information will help you with your candidate and opposition research, your campaign message, and your message box. Both major party candidates used social media; these sites should be explored.

- *District voting data.* We provide some of the information you will need to collect on the voters of the 91st District, from 2004 through 2012. Again, you may have to rely on your research skills to complement the provided information. Voting results by precinct can be found on the Michigan Secretary of State's website and the Muskegon County Clerk's website. These data will help you create a voter analysis and targeting strategy.

- *Campaign finance information.* We provide some examples of actual 2012 campaign finance reports from the two candidates. These show who the campaigns got their money from (individuals, political parties, interest group PACs) and what they spent it on. While we have tried to keep this simulation as realistic as possible, we deviate a bit from the real world here. The race for the 2012 Michigan 91st State House District was competitive; therefore, more money would likely be spent in this race than in a typical state house race. More money means more things can be done and a wider variety of tactics can be utilized. Remember also that a competitive race could attract the interest of super PACs, which might spend money for advertising on behalf of a candidate or in opposition to his or her opponent. The Michigan Secretary of State's website provides campaign finance reports for candidates in current and previous elections. In general, we want the amount of money available to your campaign to be somewhat less than what is typically spent for this kind of race in this state. We supply you with a budget figure that you will have to work with in completing some of the exercises in Chapters 3 and 4. This figure will force you to make some tough choices when completing the exercises. The real learning comes from having to divvy up scarce resources in an efficient manner. The budget you have to work with in the Michigan 91st State House District is $200,000. Campaign finance information is available on the book's companion website through the link provided for the

National Institute on Money in State Politics, and official reports are located on the Michigan Secretary of State's website. Compiling campaign finance information for this district will help you prepare a campaign budget, including a fund-raising strategy and spending decisions for communications, voter contact, and paid media. It also will help in preparing a campaign calendar.

## Wrap-up and Next Steps

The material in this chapter will provide you with much of the information and data that you will use for your campaign simulation. While we have provided background information and useful links to public information about laws, election results, and district location, the exercises outlined in Chapters 3 and 4 provide more specific instructions about how to proceed in putting together a campaign plan. We have also provided a table on the book's companion website called "Steps in Creating a Campaign Plan," which briefly summarizes the steps you should take when preparing a plan. In addition, we have left some information for you to find on your own—much as you would need to do if you were participating in an actual campaign. Good luck!

## CHAPTER 7
# VIRGINIA HOUSE OF DELEGATES DISTRICT 94

The state of Virginia holds an important place in US history. The first permanent English colony was settled in what is now Virginia. Indeed, Jamestown was chartered in 1607, thirteen years before the Pilgrims landed on Plymouth Rock. The state is considered a commonwealth, designated as such because the state's founders believed that power was held by the people and that government's purpose was to promote the "common weal," or common good. The state also is known as the "Old Dominion State," after the exalted "dominion" status given to the colony of Virginia by King Charles II (Peaslee and Swartz 2014). The state's role in the history of the United States cannot be overstated. In addition to contributions such as the "Virginia Plan," which proposed a bicameral legislature and population-based representation in the legislature at the Constitutional Convention, Virginia gave the United States a total of eight presidents, more than any other state. The Virginia State House also has served as a pathway for a number of politicians who had a major impact on the founding of an independent United States and on later national politics and government. For example, George Washington, Patrick Henry, and Thomas Jefferson all served in the Virginia House of Burgesses early in their careers of public service. Virginia is a relatively large state geographically, and it has a variety of different regions with their own cultural traditions, local economies, and political preferences. The state's western region includes parts of the Appalachian and Blue Ridge Mountain ranges, and it borders the states of West Virginia, Kentucky, Tennessee, and North Carolina. Like its neighbor to the south, North Carolina,

Virginia has a Piedmont region, the rolling hills that serve as a transition from the mountains to the coast. The Tidewater region is located in the far eastern part of the state, and its shores touch Chesapeake Bay, several major rivers, and the Atlantic Ocean. The state's northernmost cities and counties form part of the Washington, DC, metropolitan area. Because of northern Virginia's proximity to Washington, DC, this area has grown in size considerably and is populated by those who work in and around the federal government. For example, the National Rifle Association has its headquarters in Fairfax, and the National Wildlife Federation's headquarters is located in Reston.

## Virginia's Political Context

Virginia provides several examples of the axiom "states vary" with respect to their laws and practices. For example, the state holds its state-level elections in *odd-numbered years*. Virginia also has only three statewide elective offices (other than US Senate)—governor, lieutenant governor, and attorney general. The heads of all other executive branch departments are appointed by the governor. While important appointment powers reside in the governor's office, Virginia is the only state that prohibits its governors from serving consecutive terms. A governor may serve more than one four-year term, but the terms cannot be consecutive. Compare this with states such as Texas, which has no restrictions on a governor's terms, and states such as Michigan, which restricts a governor to two terms. In addition, Virginia is the only state besides South Carolina in which state judges are appointed by the state legislature rather than by gubernatorial appointment or election by citizens. Virginia also is unique in that it has a number of "independent cities"; that is, they are politically and legally independent of the county in which they are located. Alexandria, Lynchburg, Roanoke, and Newport News (where the 94th District is located) are independent cities. As part of this arrangement, residents of these cities do not pay a county tax, nor do they receive county government services. This can create odd arrangements. For example, the independent city of Fairfax also serves as the county seat of Fairfax County, but the two governments are entirely separate and independent of each other.

In contemporary presidential politics, Virginia's thirteen Electoral College votes after the 2010 census remained unchanged from the 2000 census, despite the fact that the state's population increased substantially between 2000 and 2010. According to the US Census Bureau, Virginia had an estimated population of 8,001,024 in 2010.[1] With one hundred seats in the House of Delegates, each delegate served approximately 80,100 people after the 2010 census. But the state has been an important player in presidential elections, especially in 2008 and 2012, when it was considered a battleground state and received considerable attention from the candidates and the media.

Not surprisingly, the western, more rural areas of the state tend to be more conservative and elect Republican candidates with regularity. The metropolitan areas tend to support Democratic Party candidates, but the state could probably be considered center-right when put in the context of ideology across the United States. The state has generally supported Republican presidential candidates in the past, but it was a battleground state in 2008 and 2012, and both times Democrat Barack Obama carried the state.

Newcomers to the state tend to settle in the northern Virginia area around Washington, DC, as well as the Norfolk-Virginia Beach-Hampton Roads-Newport News area. An important note for operating political campaigns in Virginia is that some of the state's growth between 2000 and 2010 was the result of immigration to the state. Reports of 2010 census data indicate that 38 percent of Virginia residents were born in another state and about 11 percent were born outside of the United States (Peaslee and Swartz 2014). The state has a relatively diverse population as well. About one in five Virginians is African-American (19.7 percent), compared to about 13 percent in the United States as a whole. About 6 percent are Asian (compared to 5 percent nationally), and about 8 percent are Hispanic (compared to 16.9 percent nationally).[2]

Virginia is known as having fairly strict election rules and laws. Until 1998, the state required 17,000 petition signatures for candidates to gain ballot access for certain races, but after 1998, the state lowered the minimum number to 10,000. But even with that lower number, all but two presidential candidates in 2012 failed to reach the Virginia Republican primary ballot. Only Mitt Romney and Ron Paul were able to obtain the minimum 10,000 registered voter signatures (including a minimum of 400 from each congressional district) needed to qualify for the primary ballot. Virginia has no provisions for early in-person voting, no-excuse absentee voting, or other election reforms that other states have enacted. In addition, the state has no provisions for citizen-initiated ballot proposals (e.g., initiatives and recalls) as California and Michigan do, although, like all states, it does allow legislative-sponsored referenda. In 2013, Virginia followed a number of other states in passing a voter identification law, which requires voters to present valid identification before they can vote. The law became effective in 2014. However, the state law also mandates that citizens be given free photo identification cards if they do not already have one, and it allows several different forms of photo identification.

A Gallup report noted that in 2013 Virginia was one of the most evenly divided states by party identification in the entire United States, with 41.1 percent of individuals indicating that they considered themselves Democratic or leaning Democratic and 42.1 percent saying they considered themselves Republican or leaning Republican.[3] Still, the state has had various swings in political power over time. For example, Virginia had a "Republican trifecta" between 2009 and 2014, when Republicans held majorities in both the state Senate and House of Delegates while also occupying the governor's office. The state also regularly sends a majority of Republicans to Washington, DC, as part of its congressional delegation. After the 2012 elections, Virginia sent three Democrats and eight Republicans to the US House (the same party breakdown as the 2010 elections), but both Virginia senators were Democrats.

Despite the recent Republican electoral successes, Virginia has been a relatively competitive state for statewide offices, electing both Republican and Democratic governors regularly over the past 30 years. Democrats were elected to the governership in the 1980s, Republicans in the 1990s, and Democrats again in 2002 and 2006. In the two most recent elections, Republican Bob McDonnell was elected in 2009, but in 2013 Democrat Terry McAuliffe narrowly defeated Republican Ken Cuccinelli in a hotly contested gubernatorial election. However, the Republican Party took a majority of House of Delegates seats in 1999 and has held on to that majority through the 2013 elections.

## Characteristics of the 94th District

In Virginia, there are one hundred House of Delegate districts, each with a target population after the 2010 census of 80,100 (see Table 7.1). The members of the chamber serve two-year terms. It is important to remember that Virginia holds its state elections in odd-numbered years—so, for example, the state held statewide and House of Delegates elections in 2013. This can be important to those who are part of a House of Delegates campaign team, since it can have a

**Table 7.1**    Virginia at a Glance

| | |
|---|---|
| 2012 state population (est.) | 8,185,867 |
| 2012 number of US congressional seats | 11 |
| Number of state Senate seats | 40 |
| Number of state delegate seats | 100 |
| 2011 state senate district population (target) | 200,000 |
| 2011 state delegate district population (target) | 80,100 |
| 2010 Delegate District 94 population | 71,464 |
| Voter registration by party | No |
| Full-time legislature | No |
| Legislative term limits | No |
| Independent redistricting commission | Advisory only |

large impact on how a campaign is run and which voters are likely to participate. Even though there may be higher-level races being held at the same time (e.g., governor, attorney general), there is no presidential election, or even a midterm election in which candidates are running for Congress. Voter turnout is likely to be different, and the kinds of voters (by age, race, gender, and other characteristics) who vote in odd-numbered years may be quite different than those who vote in presidential election years.

The Virginia House of Delegates is considered a part-time legislature, with legislative sessions lasting sixty days in even-numbered years and thirty days in odd-numbered years. Sessions begin on the second Wednesday each January. The state's governor can reconvene the legislature for a special session, and the members themselves can extend the shorter (thirty-day) session if two-thirds approve (Peaslee and Swartz 2014). As of 2013, delegates earn an annual salary of $17,640, as well as per diem compensation of $135 per day for food and expenses while they are in the state capital. The Virginia state legislature has no term limits.

The 94th District's population at the time of redistricting after the 2010 census was 71,464. The district is located within the southeastern part of the state in the city of Newport News.[4] Situated at end of the Virginia Peninsula in the Hampton Roads area along the northern shore of the James River, it is an important shipbuilding center and port. The city's estimated population in 2012 was 180,726. Therefore, the 94th District comprises a little less than half of the city of Newport News; the 93rd, 94th, and 95th delegate districts all serve parts of the city. A 2012 census report estimated that just over half of the city's population was white (at 51.1 percent), 41.3 percent were African American, 7.9 percent Hispanic, and 3.0 percent Asian.[5]

The city's large employers includes Huntington Ingalls Industries Shipbuilding Company, the Langley-Eustis US Air Force–US Army Joint Base installation, and the Newport News Marine Terminal. The Fort Eustis Military Reservation takes up a large part of the northwestern portion of the district. The district also includes the Oyster Point City Center retail and commercial development, Patrick Henry Mall, the Warwick Village Center shopping area, a satellite campus of Old Dominion University, and Christopher Newport University. There are several inlets of the James River located in the district, including the Warwick River, Deep Creek, and Lake Maury. In addition, there are several public parks along the James River in the district, including Huntington Park and the expansive Mariners' Museum and Park. The Mariners' Museum is a large facility; among many other artifacts, it displays a replica (and part of the original turret) of the Union ironclad warship USS Monitor, which battled the ironclad CSS Virginia (Merrimack) at the Battle of Hampton Roads during the Civil War. About one-quarter of the city's employed population works for the government or a government contractor, so the 2012 federal government shutdown was a significant event for the Newport News area.

There are twenty-three precincts in the 94th District, although seven of them are split (i.e., voters in one precinct are divided between two legislative districts). As such, some polling places for the 94th District are located outside the district boundaries (and serve another district as well). In Virginia, polling places are open from 6 a.m. to 7 p.m.—similar to Illinois and Missouri but an hour before polling places open and close in a number of states, including Michigan, Maryland, Delaware, and California.

## The Candidates

### David E. Yancey (R)[6]

David Yancey was first elected to the Virginia House of Delegates in 2011. He was born in Newport News and was 41 years old at the time of the 2013 campaign.

He is a Roman Catholic and unmarried with no children. He is a small business owner and entrepreneur who worked for a family business and in real estate and investments. He started his own real estate and property management business, and, later, a fishing business. He earned his bachelor's degree in political science and history from the University of Georgia in 1995.

Yancey first came to office under unusual circumstances. In 2011, the Republican Party had renominated the district's incumbent, Glenn Oder. However, in August 2011, Oder resigned from the House of Delegates to take a position as executive director of the Fort Monroe Authority, a newly created agency whose purpose was to oversee the disposal of equipment and material from Fort Monroe, a military base that recently had been closed. The 94th District Republican Committee nominated Yancey at a meeting two days after Oder's resignation. Yancey ran in the general election and won his first election in 2011. During his first term of office, he served on the Education and Transportation committees. Because a large number of his constituents serve in the military, work for the federal government, or work for a government contractor, Yancey sent a letter to all members of the Virginia congressional delegation urging them to quickly resolve the 2013 federal government shutdown (Murphy 2013).

### Robert Farinholt (D)[7]

At the time of the 2013 campaign, Robert Farinholt was a 33-year-old first-time candidate for public office. He is a firefighter and paramedic with the Hampton Roads Fire Department and comes from a long line of police officers and firefighters. He attended Woodside High School in northern Newport News. He has received specialized education and training as a paramedic as well as training from the Hampton Roads Fire Officer Command School. He ran unopposed in the June 11 Democratic primary. He and his wife are members of Gloria Dei Lutheran Church in Newport News. Farinholt's wife Tami serves as coordinator for community service at Old Dominion University's Office of Student Activities and Leadership.

Farinholt is a highly decorated firefighter who earned his department's Medal of Honor in 2007. He and his wife are regular supporters of a number of charitable organizations, including the Salvation Army and the American Society for the Prevention of Cruelty to Animals (ASPCA), along with several animal rescue shelters.

## Web Resources to Help Create a Campaign Plan

The discussion of the context surrounding the candidates for the Virginia 94th House of Delegates District campaign provides the reader with enough information to begin conducting district and demographic analyses as well as candidate profiles for the simulation and the exercises in Chapters 3 and 4. Supplemental material needed to complete those exercises is available on the book's companion website, but you also may wish to conduct your own Internet search. The Virginia Public Access Project provides a wealth of information about these elections. We provide the following information that you will use in completing the exercises in Chapters 3 and 4:

- *A map of the district.* The map shows the general boundaries of the district within the state. This map will help you to begin to familiarize yourself with the district and the lay of the land where the campaign will be waged. A detailed map of the district will show you that this is an urban district, since the entire district is located in the city of Newport News (but only part of the city comprises this district). This kind of information can help your campaign determine some aspects of the campaign strategy, such as whether the candidate and campaign volunteers will go door to door or whether you should focus on other ways to contact voters. This map will help you when you compile your district analysis.
- *US census data on the Virginia House of Delegates 94th District.* This information will be the beginning of your research into the district and the voters of the district, which you will use in several of the exercises in Chapters 3 and 4. We provide some of the information you will need, but there is more out there. For example, the Newport News community profile information compiled by the Virginia Employment Commission provides regularly updated data on the city's demographics, economics, and educational attainment. This information is mostly derived from US census data. You will have to use your research skills to go out and find other pertinent data that will help you complete the exercises. This information will help you create your district analysis.
- *News articles on the campaign.* Explore the link provided for the Virginia Public Access Project's website to view some news accounts that preview the

race and describe the candidates and their campaigns. You may also wish to visit other websites (of the candidates, of other news media, and of "good government" organizations). Websites sponsored by Project Vote Smart and Vote VA also contain useful information about the candidates and issues. Both candidates aired TV ads in 2013 and used social media as well. This information will help you with your candidate and opposition research, the campaign message, and the message box.

- *Voter data on the district.* We provide some of the information you will need to collect on the voters of the 94th District, from 2007 through 2013. Again, you may have to rely on your research skills to complement the given information. These data also are available on the Virginia State Board of Elections website. They will help you create a voter analysis and targeting strategy for the district.

- *Campaign finance information.* We provide some examples of actual campaign finance reports from the two candidates. These show where the campaigns got their money (individuals, political parties, interest group PACs) and what they spent it on. While we have tried to keep this simulation as realistic as possible, we deviate a bit from the real world here. The race for the Virginia 94th House of Delegates District is competitive; therefore, more money would likely be spent in this race than in a typical state house race. More money means more things can be done and a wider variety of tactics can be utilized. Remember also that a competitive race may spur some interest by Super PACs, which might spend money on advertising on behalf of a candidate or in opposition to his or her opponent. In general, we want the amount of money available to your campaign to be somewhat less than what is typically spent for this kind of race in this state. We supply you with a budget figure that you will have to work with in completing some of the exercises in Chapters 3 and 4. This figure will force you to make some tough choices when completing some of the exercises. The budget you have to work with in the 94th Virginia House of Delegates District race is $400,000. Campaign spending information is available from the Virginia State Board of Elections website and the National Institute for Money in State Politics. Compiling campaign finance information for this district will help you prepare a campaign budget, including a fundraising strategy and spending decisions for communications, voter contact, and paid media. It also will help in preparing a campaign calendar.

## Wrap-up and Next Steps

The material in this chapter will provide you with much of the information and data that you will use for your campaign simulation. While we have provided background information and useful links to public information about laws, election results, and district location, the exercises outlined in Chapters 3 and 4 provide more specific instructions about how to proceed in putting together a campaign plan. We have also provided a table on the book's companion website called "Steps in Creating a Campaign Plan," which briefly summarizes the steps you should take when preparing a plan. In addition, we have left some information for you to find on your own—much as you would need to do if you were participating in an actual campaign. Good luck!

## CHAPTER 8
## CALIFORNIA ASSEMBLY DISTRICT 60

The state of California is a powerhouse in politics, government, and elections. It is the most populous state in the nation, which means it also has the most members of the US House of Representatives (fifty-three) as well as the most Electoral College votes in the presidential selection process (fifty-five). After the 2012 elections, the state sent thirty-eight Democrats and fifteen Republicans to the US House. In the 113th Congress that began in January 2013, Representative Kevin McCarthy (R-23) served as Majority Whip and, beginning in August 2014, as Majority Leader. Representative Nancy Pelosi (D-12) served as House Minority Leader in the 113th Congress, and she also became the first female Speaker of the House in US history in January 2007, the last time Democrats controlled the House. In 2013, Ann Ravel, Chair of the California Fair Practices Political Commission, was appointed by President Obama to serve as a member of the Federal Election Commission, which administers and enforces federal campaign finance law. The state also produced the first modern political consultants, Clem Whitaker and Leone Baxter, who started Campaigns Inc. in 1933 and went on to work for a lengthy list of notable candidates and causes.[1] Finally, California has given us US Presidents Ronald Reagan and Richard Nixon, both Republicans.

## California's Political Context

For many years, California has been a state that attracts immigrants, which has influenced the state's overall culture and, more specifically, its political culture.

The state witnessed a great influx of immigrants during the Gold Rush of the 1840s and 1850s. These immigrants mostly came from the eastern part of the United States, but some came directly from other countries. The construction of the Southern Pacific Railroad brought many Chinese immigrants in the mid- to late-1800s. In the twentieth century, successive waves of immigrants came to California seeking opportunity during the Great Depression, jobs in aviation and defense during World War II, and filmmaking and technology boom jobs in the postwar period (Ting, Stambough, and Arsenault 2011).

Most recently, migration from Asia and Latin America also has helped to shape the culture of California. These waves of immigration to the state have influenced the state's politics and its economy, and they have combined to create a diverse population unlike almost any other state in the United States. The state's 2012 population estimate of over 38 million people is the largest of any state, and it continues to grow, with an estimated 2.1 percent population increase between April 2010 and July 2012. Moreover, no single racial or ethnic group constitutes a majority of the population. Californians considered to be what the US Census Bureau calls "white alone" (i.e., no other race) comprised 39.4 percent of the 2012 population, followed closely by Hispanic/Latinos at 38.2 percent, Asians at 13.9 percent, and African Americans at 6.6 percent.[2] Indeed, California was one of the earliest states to have become a "majority-minority" population—that is, the combined minority populations of the state exceed the white population.

California has been active in adopting election reforms designed to increase voter participation and convenience, including early in-person voting and permanent no-excuse absentee balloting. The state was an early adopter of no-excuse absentee voting and is one of about five states that has added a further level of convenience to no-excuse absentee voting: Voters may apply for "permanent" absentee voting status, which means absentee ballots are automatically sent to the voter without the need to reapply. In California, such permanent status ends only if the voter fails to vote in four consecutive statewide general elections.[3] These changes in the state's election laws have a direct impact on political campaigns because they affect a campaign's plans and timetables for contacting voters, any strategy for GOTV mobilization efforts, and the overall campaign calendar. California's no-excuse law has made it much easier for voters to cast absentee ballots, and it appears it is having an impact. The California Secretary of State's office has calculated that 51.2 percent of California voters voted by absentee ballot in the 2012 general election, and almost two-thirds of primary voters (65.2 percent) voted absentee in the primary that year.[4] Because of these reforms, political campaigns must adjust any strategy that assumes most voters will be voting at a polling place on a single Election Day.

In 2012, California also began using a "top-two" primary voting system, whereby the two candidates of any party receiving the most votes in the primary go on to run in the general election. In a number of cases, this has meant that two Republicans or two Democrats have run against each other in a district's general election. This can drastically affect a campaign's plan and overall strategy because it makes it more likely that a candidate will need to appeal to independent voters, and possibly voters affiliated with another party. Among other outcomes, this may produce winning candidates with more moderate views than in previous elections.

As with other states, California has campaign finance regulations for its state-level candidates, along with limits imposed on direct contributions made to candidate committees (Gerston and Christensen 2013). For example, individual contributions to a state legislative race are limited to $4,100 per primary and general election. Political parties have no campaign contribution limits imposed on them, and state and local party committees of the two major parties contributed $37.7 million to all races in California during the 2012 elections.[5] The state also has an option for assembly candidates to accept voluntary spending limits for their specific race, which in the 2012 general election was $909,000.[6]

There are several important dynamics that are useful for understanding politics in California. These dynamics provide an important context for anyone campaigning for a state assembly seat. In presidential politics, California is now considered to be reliably "blue," because a majority of the state's voters have supported the Democratic Party's presidential candidates in every election since 1992. This has meant that California is not regarded as a battleground state, and as such it does not typically see many visits by candidates seeking the support of voters during a presidential campaign. However, the state is relatively wealthy, so candidates often travel to California for fund-raising events. In fact, campaign contributions made by California sources in the 2012 presidential race ($62.8 million) far outpaced the state with the next largest total (New York at $37.0 million).[7]

California has the most significant use of ballot initiatives and referenda of any state. This is due in part to its relatively lower entry costs to place proposals on the ballot. In California, to place a statute proposal or veto referendum on the ballot, petitioners need to collect enough valid signatures to equal 5 percent of the most recent gubernatorial vote total. For constitutional amendment proposals, petitioners need 8 percent of the most recent gubernatorial vote.[8] This is a low threshold for ballot proposal access compared to many other states. First, not all states even allow citizen-initiated ballot proposals (for example, two of our other case states—Texas and Virginia—do not). Second, some states have higher thresholds for ballot access. This includes Michigan, which requires 8 percent of their most recent gubernatorial vote totals for statutes and 10 percent for constitutional amendments. Other states require even more signatures— Mississippi requires 12 percent of their governor's race totals and Wyoming requires 15 percent of the vote totals in the most recent election (although not necessarily the governor's race).

One consequence of this is that California typically has many proposals on the ballot during each election. For example, California voters saw twenty-eight different ballot proposals in 1990 alone, and recent elections have seen a relatively large number of proposals as well—twelve in 2008, fourteen in 2010, and thirteen in 2012. The topics of these proposals vary widely. They include technical issues, such as Proposition 13 in 2010, which mandated that seismic retrofitting should not add to a property's tax assessed value. They also include many public borrowing and bond measures, along with tax policy proposals.[9]

Some ballot measures have a direct impact on campaigns and elections. California's term limit rules were established in 1990 by Proposition 140. The initial limits for assembly members provided for a maximum of three two-year terms. However, Proposition 28 in 2012 allowed anyone elected in 2012 or later to serve twelve years in the state legislature in any combination of senate and assembly terms. Through other state initiatives, California voters have approved reforms such as the top-two primary and a Citizens Redistricting Commission with full power to redraw voting districts after each census.[10]

In 1966, the state adopted a "professional legislature" model in which members work full time year-round and have a staff large enough to support their legislative duties. Arguably, this makes the legislature more of an equal policy-making partner with the governor. Legislators could become policy experts over time, and public service could be a career. Later, along with term limits, voters also cut resources for legislative staffs. So while members have continued to work year-round since 1990, the balance of power in state government has shifted toward the governor.

Campaigns in California are challenging for several reasons. Some are typical of modern campaigns, but other features are unique to California. For example, candidates and their campaign committees cannot ignore the more than 50 percent of the voting population that now votes by absentee ballot. This percentage represents common absentee voters such as senior citizens and those who vote this way because of the state's relaxed no-excuse absentee rules. Because the state also provides for early in-person voting, this extends the number of voting days and complicates GOTV strategies for political campaigns.

## Characteristics of the 60th District

There are eighty state assembly districts in California, each with an average population of almost half a million people (see Table 8.1). Despite its size, we selected California as a case chapter in part because it has voter registration by party, which makes some of the campaigning tasks easier. Moreover, California is an interesting state because of its use of election reforms such as permanent no-excuse voting and the top-two primary. Because of its size, the state is somewhat unusual in that lower chamber districts in other states might have closer to 100,000 or less in population. In this way, California Assembly races are more

**Table 8.1**    California at a Glance

| | |
|---|---|
| 2012 state population (est.) | 38,041,430 |
| 2012 number of US congressional seats | 53 |
| Number of state senate seats | 40 |
| Number of state assembly seats | 80 |
| 2011 state senate district population (target) | 931,349 |
| 2011 state assembly district population (target) | 465,274 |
| 2010 Assembly District 60 population | 470,287 |
| Voter registration by party | Yes |
| Full-time legislature | Yes |
| Legislative term limits | Yes |
| Independent redistricting commission | Yes |

similar to many state senate races than other state legislative campaigns. In fact, California Assembly districts are three times the size of Texas House districts, which are the next biggest House districts among state legislatures. Therefore, compared to other states, some elements of state assembly campaigns—for example, campaign fund-raising and spending demands—in California will likely be much more challenging than campaigns in other states.

As of 2012, the 60th Assembly District's population was 470,287—slightly above the targeted population of 465,274. Assembly district boundaries in 2011 were substantially different from the 2001 boundaries. After the last round of redistricting, the area now in the 60th District included parts of two assembly districts—the 66th and 71st Districts. The previous 66th District included Mira Loma and parts of the city of Riverside but stretched down through southwestern parts of Riverside County and south into San Diego County. The 71st District comprised much of the current 60th District and included Corona, Norco, and parts of the city of Riverside. But it also extended into large parts of Orange County, including Mission Viejo. Recent voter registration figures in the current 60th District show it to be fairly evenly divided. Just before the 2012 elections, district voter registrations by party were divided as follows—35.53 percent Democratic, 40.94 percent Republican, and 18.90 percent no party preference (voter registrations are regularly updated, so the percentages change frequently).[11] There are 141 precincts in the 60th Assembly District. The district is east and south of Los Angeles and is part of what is known as the "Inland Empire."

The district is located in the northwestern part of Riverside County. The entire county had a 2012 estimated population of about 2.2 million, and it was the fourth most populous county in California after the 2010 census. The district's major employers include several school districts, such as the Corona-Norco Unified School District, the Alvord Unified School District, and the Jurupa Unified School District. The Corona Regional Medical Center is a major health care facility in the district. There also are two prison facilities—the California Rehabilitation Center in Norco, and the California Institution for Women, located in Corona. The district's commuters are served by I-15, which runs north and south and generally bisects the district. The Santa Ana River forms part of the boundary line in the northeastern part of the district.

Corona, with a 2012 estimated population of about 158,000 people, is one of the district's larger communities (and comprises a large portion of the 60th District, along with the western part of the city of Riverside). Smaller communities include Norco (which calls itself "Horsetown, USA" and has a more rural feel), Eastvale, El Cerrito, and Jurupa Valley. Outside but near the district, the region includes the cities of San Bernardino and Ontario.

## The Candidates

### Eric Linder (R)[12]

Eric Linder's first attempt at elective office came with his 2012 campaign for the California 60th Assembly District seat. At the time of the 2012 election, Linder was relatively young—just thirty-three years old. Eric is the son of a Mexican immigrant father and lives in Corona, a growing city in the district with a population of about 158,000.[13] He attended schools in the area, including Highland Elementary and Norco High School. He has lived most of his life in the 60th Assembly District and is proud that he is raising his family in the same area where he grew up.

For many years, Linder worked in the real estate industry, and he later founded an online communications company. He also previously owned and operated an aircraft rental and chartering company. As a small business owner, he has had considerable concern over high taxes and was a founder of the Corona Taxpayers Association. A major feature of his 2012 campaign was his pledge that he would never vote for a tax increase. During the 2012 campaign, Linder signed the Americans for Tax Reform "Taxpayer Protection Pledge," which was sponsored by the national anti-tax organization led by Grover Norquist. Linder has been active in Republican Party politics for a number of years. For example, he has served as the vice-chair of the Riverside County Republican Party and was a founding member of the Riverside County Young Republicans organization. In addition, his online communications firm has built websites for several members of the Republican Assembly Caucus.

In addition to his strong stand against taxes, he regards crime-fighting policies as a top priority. He took positions against the state's proposed high-speed rail project during the 2012 campaign but supported fixing the state's old water delivery system (i.e., more reservoirs and water storage infrastructure). He was in favor of eliminating California's version of the DREAM Act. He was in favor of balancing the state's budget and supporting small and growing businesses. He also was concerned about the growing legacy costs in the state's pension system.

## Jose Luis Perez (D)[14]

Jose Luis Perez is a resident of Riverside and a long-time resident of the 60th Assembly District. At age seventy, he is retired from a career in public education. While running for state assembly, Perez was serving as president of the Alvord Unified School District Board of Education. He has served as an elected member of the Alvord Board of Education for twenty-one years. Perez earned an associate of science degree in business and a bachelor of science degree in business and management. He completed his formal education at California State University, San Bernardino, earning an MA in education. Earlier in his career, he served as a public school teacher in the Fontana Unified School District (from 1991 to 1995).

As a part of Perez's campaign, he proposed to create a Citizen's Advisory Panel composed of representatives from every city in the 60th Assembly District. The proposed panel would hold hearings, conduct studies, and prepare recommendations for improvements for the district. His campaign promised to focus on attracting quality employers to the district to increase jobs for citizens and to work to extend the opportunity for all to receive a quality and affordable education. While noting that he was a lifelong Democrat, Perez announced his willingness to work with all parties, ethnic groups, and age groups. His campaign promised that he would eliminate waste in all areas of government, promote efficiency across all government programs, put in place a fair and proportional income tax program, and help create policies that would be friendly to business, industry, manufacturing, and commerce enterprises. He favors tax incentives to businesses that meet the needs of both the company and the community. In keeping with his background as an educator, he strongly supports K–12 education as well as funding for colleges and universities. He considers himself a "citizen legislator" and has indicated that he does not want to be a career politician.

## Web Resources to Help Create a Campaign Plan

The discussion of the context surrounding the candidates for the California 60th Assembly District campaign provides the reader with enough information to begin conducting district and demographic analyses as well as candidate profiles for the simulation and the exercises in Chapters 3 and 4. Supplemental material needed to complete those exercises is available on the book's companion website, where you will find redistricting information, campaign finance reports, voter data, party registration information, and news articles on the 2012 election. You may also wish to conduct your own Internet search for information and data helpful to your research.

However, remember that the resources provided to you provide specific data that were available for the 2012 election cycle, so when conducting the simulation in future years you will have to make sure to get updated information to complete items such as your analysis of the district, candidates, issues, and even budgets. The information provided here and online that you will use in completing the exercises in Chapters 3 and 4 includes:

- *A map of the district.* The map included on the book's companion website shows the general boundaries of the district. It also provides important information in terms of where the district is situated in relation to other communities in the area. A more detailed map of the district can tell you what kind of district in which you will be working—urban, rural, suburban, or a combination of the three. That kind of map can also help you determine some aspects of campaign strategy such as whether the candidate will go door to door or whether canvassing of this kind is out of the question because of the district's geographic elements. This will help you create a district analysis.
- *US census data on the California 60th Assembly District.* Selected information from the US Census Bureau will be the beginning of your research into the district and the voters of the district, which you will use in several of the exercises in Chapters 3 and 4. We provide you with some of the census data on communities within the district, but there is more out there. These data will help you create a district analysis. You will have to use your research skills to go out and find other pertinent data that will help you complete the exercises.
- *News articles on the campaign.* An online newspaper covering this district is the *Press Enterprise*. Online sources such as Project Vote Smart or Ballotpedia also provide biographical material about the candidates, along with a short description of the issues. These will be useful in several of the exercises. This information will help you with candidate and opposition research for this district and with creating a message box.
- *District voting data.* We provide some of the information you will need to collect on the voters of the 60th District. Again, you may have to rely on your research skills to complement the given information. These data from the California Secretary of State and the Riverside County Clerk will help you

create a voter analysis, which you will use to calculate the number of votes you will need to win the election.

- *Campaign finance information.* We provide some examples of actual campaign finance reports from the two candidates. These show where the campaigns got their money and what they spent it on. The race for the California 60th Assembly District is competitive; therefore, more money likely would be spent in this race than in a state assembly race that is not competitive. The budget figure we provide will force you to make tough choices when completing some of the exercises. The budget you have to work with in the California 60th Assembly District is $500,000. While this may seem like a lot of money, the median amount of money spent by winners in 2012 was almost $600,000. This will help you prepare a campaign budget, including a fund-raising strategy and spending decisions for communications, voter contact, and paid media. It also will help in preparing a campaign calendar.

## Wrap-up and Next Steps

The material in this chapter will provide you with much of the information and data needed for your campaign simulation. While we have provided background information and useful links to public information about laws, election results, and district location, the exercises outlined in Chapters 3 and 4 provide more specific instructions about how to proceed in putting together a campaign plan. We have also provided a table on the book's companion website called "Steps in Creating a Campaign Plan," which briefly summarizes the steps you should take when preparing a plan. In addition, we have left some information for you to find on your own—much as you would need to do if you were participating in an actual campaign. Good luck!

## CHAPTER 9
# STATE HOUSE CAMPAIGNS IN A NATIONAL CONTEXT

Creating and faithfully executing a realistic campaign plan is central to all well-run political campaigns, regardless of the office being sought. Our approach in this book has been to focus on how campaigns operate in state legislative races, and more particularly, state house races. We believe that campaigns for the state house provide excellent illustrations of political campaigns at all levels, including federal elections. While there are many differences between federal races and those farther down the ballot, there also are many similarities. At the same time, almost all state house races are small enough to be manageable for purposes of this campaign simulation and the associated exercises that we have presented in this book. It is much easier to manage a state house race that has 80,000 (in Virginia) or 90,000 (in Michigan) residents compared to the 710,000 residents who live in an average US House district. However, we believe that many of the principles employed when campaigning for a state house race also can be applied in a US House campaign.

We believe an important element of understanding down-ballot campaigns is to note the influence of national-level forces on these lower-level races. State politics operates within a national context, and specific campaigns operating in particular years may be very much affected by the larger forces of economics and politics at the national level. We believe that former US House Speaker Tip O'Neill's famous adage—"all politics is local"[1]—does apply to campaigns, but that national forces can play a large role in down-ballot races as well. Of course, national and local concerns merge in certain situations. For example, the federal government shutdown during the first two weeks of October 2013 was an important local issue for many in Virginia's 94th state House of Delegates district in Newport News. Because the district has a large military installation and a shipbuilding company with federal contracts, the federal shutdown had a tremendous impact on the local economy and on families living in the 94th District. As such, Republican incumbent David Yancey broke ranks with many Republican elected officials around the United States by sending a letter to all members of the Virginia US Congressional delegation, asking them to "put aside partisan differences" and resolve the federal shutdown (Murphy 2013).

Larger economic and political trends can equally influence voter attitude and mood regarding candidates of different political parties and philosophies or whether incumbents should be reelected. If the US economy is doing well at the time of an election, incumbents tend to be rewarded with reelection. If the economy is doing poorly, challengers have a potentially more effective message of "change." If a sitting president does not have very high job approval ratings and the national unemployment rate is high, candidates of the president's party up and down the ballot have a much more difficult time winning election. This was the case in the 2006, 2008, and 2010 elections.

Of course, issues specific to each state and district will play a role in determining the outcome of state house elections. Indeed, states have become more prominent in national politics, especially as many Republican governors have openly challenged Democratic President Barack Obama on a number of issues. While there have been examples of federal preemption during the early part of the twenty-first century (e.g., the No Child Left Behind Act), federal dominance beginning in the 1930s began to wane in a more obvious way with Republican Ronald Reagan's election in 1980. In addition, Democratic President Bill Clinton attempted to decrease the size and power of the federal government, which was reflected in his 1996 State of the Union message that proclaimed "the era of big government is over."[2] Moreover, Barack Obama's "progressive federalism" approach has allowed states to exceed minimum federal standards in such areas as environmental policy (Gray, Hanson, and Kousser 2013). In turn, states have begun to emerge as more important players in the US federated system.

## Similarities between State and National Elections

One of the themes of this book is that on some important dimensions, state-level campaigns and elections are quite similar to those for US Congress and for president. For example, the role of parties and partisanship remains crucial for both levels—despite the fact that more and more voters seem to have weaker partisan attachments when compared to thirty and forty years ago. The party label on a ballot still acts as a voting cue for many voters, and parties still play a formal role in nominating their candidates in primary elections.

Incumbency remains important to the outcomes of both state and federal elections, although it, too, has suffered somewhat in more recent years. For example, even with the major wave elections in 2006, 2008, and 2010, a large majority of incumbents who ran for reelection were returned to office in those years. In 2006 and 2008, 94 percent of US House incumbents were reelected, while 85 percent were reelected in the 2010 midterm elections. However, public opinion polls have revealed an anti-incumbency mood among voters over the past ten years, particularly for Congress. A 2014 Gallup poll indicated that only 19 percent of voters believe that most members of Congress deserve to be reelected (Newport 2014). Despite an anti-incumbency mood among some voters, incumbents typically enjoy wide name recognition and an ability to raise campaign funds, and they have experience from previous elections in putting together a winning coalition of voters.

Partisanship and incumbency are often featured in combination when considering another similarity shared by state and federal campaigns—the redistricting advantages of majority party incumbents. Every ten years, legislatures in most states redraw voting district boundaries for all offices in their state, as required by federal law and various US Supreme Court decisions. In many cases, legislatures have drawn a large majority of "safe" districts favoring one party's candidates over the other's.

Campaign spending is crucial for all levels of elections. While spending more money does not guarantee a win, the importance of money cannot be overstated. Raising more money allows a candidate to purchase more electioneering activities. For example, they can pay more staff, purchase polling services, and communicate more with voters through radio or TV advertisements, social media, telephone calls, direct mail, or brochures and polling place literature. The cost of running successful campaigns has increased at all levels of political office, even though the advent of social media has allowed campaigns to communicate with followers in an inexpensive way. Campaigns at almost all levels tend to see a similar spending pattern, where there likely are substantial spending differences between candidates running for the same office. Incumbents tend to have a distinct advantage when raising campaign funds compared to challengers. Differences in spending tend to occur in noncompetitive races and in safe districts, but even in our 2012 California 60th Assembly District election example, the winning candidate spent over ten times the amount of money spent by the losing candidate. At the same time, campaigns at all levels are seeing increases in the amounts of money spent by groups other than the candidate committees themselves. These groups include super PACs, 501(c)(4) groups, traditional PACs, and, in selected races, political parties.

## Differences between State and National Elections

In our discussion regarding similarities between national and state campaigns and elections, we presented a picture painted in fairly broad strokes. While it is true there are a number of commonalities between state and national elections, several important differences of degree emerge when conducting a more detailed comparison. For example, all campaigns seek media attention, but the media pays the most attention to a presidential campaign. As we move down the ballot, less and less media attention is given to an election. With less media attention comes less interest and knowledge among voters. Down-ballot races are less salient to voters, and voter turnout falls for these elections. A presidential race commonly increases voter turnout, although there can be ballot roll-off for lower-level races in presidential election years. When elections are held with no presidential race, voter turnout usually is lower, as is common for midterm elections. In Virginia, predicting turnout in a House of Delegates race can be even more complicated, since the state holds both statewide and delegate elections in odd-numbered years.

In addition to differences in media attention, salience, and voter turnout, down-ballot races typically have fewer resources with which to campaign. With very little media attention and without the resources to spend on paid media, state house campaigns often cannot capture the attention and interest of voters. As such, voters know little about the characteristics or individual qualities of candidates who run for state-level legislative offices, so incumbency, name recognition, and a party label often become important factors. In this respect, state house races still resemble old-fashioned party-centered politics, in terms of the party label on the ballot (and in ads) serving as a voting cue for voters. Moreover, these races tend to be more labor intensive than higher-level races, relying much more on a candidate's personal contact with voters along with campaign volunteers.

As we have noted, campaign communication principles are similar across all campaigns and elections. Effective campaigns create a campaign message and communicate that message to as many voters as possible. However, campaigns with fewer resources are much more limited in their ability to capture the attention of potential voters. Most state house campaigns cannot afford to purchase airtime on television, or if they can, they are limited to cable television ads. In most cases, it is not likely that a campaign for state house will run very many ads, even if they can afford television. It is more common that state house campaigns will rely on direct mail literature and personal contact opportunities to communicate with voters, through social media and door-to-door campaigning or face-to-face meetings with homeowners or civic groups.

Social media is a possible answer for those campaigning in a state house campaign on limited resources. After all, it is basically free to set up a campaign Facebook page or post a video on YouTube, and it is inexpensive to communicate to followers via Twitter once an account has been established. State house campaigns also can use social media to inexpensively communicate with and mobilize volunteers. However, the same challenge exists with social media as it always has with traditional media: Are people paying attention to what you are saying? The competition for voter attention has never been more intense or difficult. A candidate for state house is competing not just against their opponent for voter attention, but against all other campaigns. Moreover, there is a vast amount of nonpolitical communication that also is vying for attention—TV shows, online videos, celebrity news, video games, social media, music, and the myriad of other distractions now available.

## Variation across States

In addition to the differences between state and national elections with respect to the factors noted above, there often are substantial differences among state-level campaigns. This is particularly true when it comes to campaign fund-raising and spending. For example, state house candidates can vary widely in the amounts of money they raise—even when running in the same district.

An examination of the politics, elections laws, and each state's political context contained in our case chapters quickly reveals a substantial diversity in how states operate. In terms of election law and administration alone, the four states we have presented provide us with a variety of rules and processes that illustrate variation across states. For example, about 40 percent of all US states have term limits for their state legislators, including our case states of California and Michigan. Our case state of Virginia elects House members in odd-numbered years, as does New Jersey. Over half of US states have early voting election reforms such as no-excuse absentee voting (California) and early in-person voting (Texas). In Virginia, polls are open on Election Day from 6 a.m. to 7 p.m., but in Michigan, polls are open between 7 a.m. and 8 p.m. This might appear to be a small detail, but it is extremely important for a campaign operating in each of those states to know when the polls are open!

With so much variation possible across states, election administration dynamics are often unique in each state. California represents an interesting case politically, in part because it has enacted a number of election procedures unlike virtually all other states. First, the state has created a Citizens Redistricting Commission, which has full authority to draw voting district boundaries. The California Assembly no longer has these powers. Second, the state holds top-two primaries, in which the top two primary election candidates run in the general election—even if they are from the same party. Third, the state allows voters to apply for a permanent no-excuse absentee ballot. This means that, after an initial application and regular participation in elections, a California voter can vote via absentee ballot in all elections—without ever reapplying or needing an excuse.

In addition, California vigorously uses its state ballot initiative system. In some elections, there may be ten or more initiatives on the ballot in California. The topics vary widely, but many of these initiatives are important to the state's political process and policy making. A number of state bond measures have been placed on the ballot in recent years. Many of the state's current reforms were approved by voters though a ballot initiative, including term limits for state legislators and the creation of the Citizens Redistricting Commission.

Virginia is unique among our case states in how it operates its elections. It holds its state house elections every two years, but its elections for statewide offices (i.e., governor, lieutenant governor, and attorney general) also are held in odd-numbered years, which can influence state house races. Interestingly, Virginia prohibits its governors from serving consecutive terms. In addition, only Virginia and South Carolina have their state legislatures appoint state judges—in most states, the governor appoints the judges or they are directly elected by voters.

Michigan is one of a minority of US states that has not enacted any of the more recent election reforms such as early in-person voting, no-excuse absentee voting, and Election Day registration. However, in 1975 the state was the first to allow citizens to register to vote at a Secretary of State's office while renewing their driver's license. This reform predated the 1993 National Voter Registration Act reform (i.e., "Motor Voter") by about twenty years.

Texas also offers a unique set of election laws. For example, Texas has offered early in-person voting opportunities to its voters for a number of years. Its bedrock conservative values include a fairly strict law-and-order sentiment. For example, the state does not allow those in prison, on probation, or on parole to vote. Texas has the largest number of ineligible voters because of these restrictions.

## The Campaign and Campaign Plan

Any political campaign must start with a candidate's decision to run. Ideally, this is an informed decision that considers not only the individual's (and his or her family's) commitment to public service but also the time required to mount an effective campaign. The campaign season is intense, from the time a candidate files to run for office until the primary election, and then again between the primary and general elections.

Aside from personal considerations that will influence a candidate's decision to run, some preliminary research about the district and the district's voters should be conducted. Knowing a great deal about a district is crucial. The best candidates are those who know a voting district intimately. They know not only the physical and geographic characteristics of a district, but also its major employers, the high schools and churches, and its civic groups. Voters often are looking for a candidate who knows the area's circumstances—both the positives and negatives of their communities. A candidate who authentically knows and understands the district in which they are running for office will have a major advantage over any opponent who does not. Among the conditions of a district that might be important are the age and condition of housing in the area; the quality of the area's infrastructure (roads, bridges, streetlights); how public spaces such as public parks and open spaces are used; the location and condition of schools; the names and locations of places of worship; and the location and types of existing businesses. County governments may also provide useful information (usually drawn from census data) on their service area, or more detailed information might be available through an area's council of governments. In some locations, groups such as the local United Way of America chapter may have sponsored a community needs assessment, which provides considerable information on possible issues or concerns felt by residents.

Knowing a district also involves conducting an analysis of a district's voting history. After all, a district may favor one party so heavily that it would be unwise for a candidate of the other party to mount a campaign. At the same time, even if a district's partisan makeup favors a candidate's party, it is possible that there will be a lot of competition in the primary since many individuals could see the same opportunity and favorable electoral context. This could be the case especially in an open-seat race. While a campaign will undertake a district and voting history analysis as part of their campaign plan, an early collection and analysis of these kinds of data will help a potential candidate decide whether to run or not. While this analysis need not be a full-blown examination of district and voting history data, it should provide enough information for a candidate to determine whether running for office in this district is feasible. This decision partly involves knowing whether an incumbent is running and whether the incumbent is popular with voters or may be vulnerable to a challenge.

This decision-making process also involves an examination of the larger political and economic context, which may or may not work in a potential candidate's favor. A good economy around election time will likely favor the party in power at the time—as well as incumbents running for reelection. A poor economy may provide opportunities for challengers or those of the minority party to craft effective campaign messages in support of their own candidacy and critical of an opponent. The larger environment can also include a political dimension. In these days of sophisticated political marketing, political parties seek to establish—and are thought of as having—a particular "brand." That is, voters likely have a perception about a particular party—and, by extension, any of its candidates. If a party has positive associations among voters, any candidate running under that label will have an advantage. Any commonly held negative associations will be a detriment to a party's candidates. For example, the Republican Party's brand suffered some blows during 2012 due to the portrayal of Republican presidential candidate Mitt Romney as elitist and uncaring. In 2013, a federal government shutdown led by the Republican-majority House also damaged the Republican Party's brand. Of course, the Democratic Party brand has had challenges over the years as well. Major flaws in the Obamacare website rollout in 2013 made the party look ineffective and indecisive. A potential candidate should have some idea of how his or her party's brand is viewed by voters, as this may affect their decision to run—or at least it will likely influence how they craft their campaign message once they starting creating a campaign plan. These national-level brands may be supplemented—or even counteracted —by the activities and perceived successes or failures of elected officials in each state. These and other factors comprise what is considered to be the context of a campaign. While the context cannot be changed at the campaign level, two campaign experts have noted that any "political strategy is largely meaningless until the context is understood" (Burton and Shea 2010, 33). Knowing the advantages and disadvantages provided by a campaign's context allows a potential candidate to make a more informed decision about running for office and provides a solid foundation on which to build a campaign plan.

### Campaign Plan

Once a campaign's context is understood and a decision to run for office has been made, a campaign should begin to craft a campaign plan. A plan is important for the smooth operation of a campaign as well as the most efficient and effective use of the limited resources a campaign will have available. Once a candidate files to run for office, a campaign can be an intense and chaotic experience. A campaign plan lays out a path and direction, helping the campaign team avoid making spur-of-the-moment decisions that could hurt a candidate's chances of winning.

A plan serves to organize a campaign team and its activities, it lays out which team members have which responsibilities, and it provides a timetable within which all activities will be accomplished. Without a plan, a campaign is much more likely to only react to events, never taking control of a campaign message, unable to deliver a consistent campaign message, and allowing their opponent to define them. Without a plan, it is more likely that a campaign will not know how much it will need to raise and spend in order to win the election, or what to do if it runs out of money. Campaigns for state house are much more likely to need volunteers for a wide variety of activities. A campaign plan will help lay out a plan to both recruit volunteers and use them effectively.

### Crisis Management

Many campaigns will find themselves in a constant state of chaos throughout the campaign season. The more prepared a campaign team is for the inevitable crisis, the better it will be able to handle the clutter and chaos. This book addresses this challenge in two ways. First, we emphasize the importance of developing and executing a campaign plan, because it can provide guidance and stability throughout a campaign. Second, we offer some crisis management exercises that we hope will allow campaign teams to understand some possible obstacles they may face. The exercises will help build skills in quickly dealing with crises but also help make those new to campaigns more aware that crises can—and will—occur.

We believe both the campaign plan and crisis management training are important to a well-managed political campaign. The campaign plan serves as the foundation for those activities and events that a campaign can control (but remember that without a plan, there is very little control). At the same time, there are activities and events that a campaign cannot anticipate. With so many volunteers and campaign staffers with little or no experience, mistakes often are made. The candidate might make an embarrassing statement or a campaign volunteer's improper actions may become public. In addition, events may occur that are simply beyond the control of a campaign. These include the actions of those on the opponent's campaign team but also those events that we have considered part of a campaign's context. The economy can improve or decline, a natural disaster can occur, or a scandal associated with one political party can emerge during a campaign. Each of these contextual factors could help or damage a campaign.

Crises will very likely occur—what is important is how quickly and effectively a campaign can respond to those crises. We included a wide variety of crisis management exercises that present scenarios a state legislative campaign might face. There is not necessarily one correct answer to the problems presented in these exercises. However, we believe that the situations presented can help campaign team members be more alert to the reality that problems can arise, and to develop some decision-making skills that will improve the team's chances of responding in a positive and effective manner. Political campaigns have been described as "organized chaos." With a well-crafted campaign plan and skills in handling crises, a campaign can increase the organized part of a campaign and reduce the effects of the chaos.

## Campaign Ethics

Campaign ethics is a potential issue in all political campaigns, whether at the national or state level. Many campaigns have candidates or volunteers for whom winning the election means everything. Sometimes those individuals will there-fore do anything to win the election. As such, we have included campaign ethics exercises in this book. The scenarios involving ethical dilemmas that we have presented seek to present real-life situations that may confront a candidate or campaign team. We find these exercises helpful because we believe that everyone will agree that campaign activists should act ethically—at least in the abstract. It may be another matter when those same people are in the throes of a heated campaign. There could be several ethical challenges during a campaign where people will have to make difficult decisions about how to act. Just remember that many average citizens dislike politics because they consider it dirty or think politi-cians lie just to get elected or believe there is too much negativity in campaigns. Winning ethically is the greatest accomplishment in politics. Political campaigns often are derided—and some campaigns deserve the criticism they receive. But campaigns can also be quite positive. They bring together like-minded people who work together to achieve a common goal. They often provide a vision for the future and ideas about how to accomplish that vision. They can be inspiring and uplifting, and they can fill people with hope. At the very least, a candidate who chooses to run for office—and does so in an ethical way—serves democracy whether they win or lose. Campaigns and elections are one of the major pathways to meaningful political action and influence, and fair and competitive elections are a foundation of American democratic theory and practice.

## Conclusion

We hope this book has provided readers with the tools to participate in the electoral pathway of American politics—and perhaps even to run for office. Political participation has the potential to bring our democratic system to life. The principles of democratic theory are most meaningful when they are put into practice. This requires citizens to become involved—by being informed, through regular voting, and perhaps by becoming active in a political campaign.

While politics often is viewed negatively by average citizens, political cam-paigns also can bring out the best that our democracy has to offer. Those who participate on a campaign team work together to support their candidate and to pursue the issues about which they are most passionate. A candidate can inspire people by promoting a vision for a better future. Campaigns offer the possibility of important issues being debated and deliberated in a serious and thoughtful way. In addition, campaigns offer citizens an opportunity to select representatives to make policy decisions on their behalf. In order to keep those representatives accountable, we hold elections on a regular basis. In many respects, political campaigns are an ideal blend of democratic theory and practice.

# Notes

## Preface

1. See *Citizens United v. Federal Election Commission*, 558 US 310 (2010), http://www.supremecourt.gov/opinions/09pdf/08-205.pdf, and *McCutcheon v. Federal Election Commission*, 572 US _____ (2014).

## Chapter 1

1. Collene Lamonte's pathway story was recounted by Collene in interviews with the authors on October 30, 2013, and January 30, 2014.

2. The impact of gerrymandering is beyond the scope of this book, but it has been studied by many scholars. See, for example, Abramowitz (1983), Cain (1985), Cox and Katz (2002), Herron and Wiseman (2008), and McCarty, Poole, and Rosenthal (2009). In addition, the role of race in gerrymandering is often important; see Hill (1995), Lublin (1997), Cameron et al. (1996), and Griggs and Katz (2005).

3. See, for example, Troy (1991), Jackson and Crotty (2001), Mayer and Bernstein (2012), Polsby et al. (2011), Sides, Epstein, and O'Halloran (2013), Medvic (2013), Pomper (2001), Wayne (2012), Campbell (2000), Holbrook (1996), or Miller and Gronbeck (1994) for presidential elections, and Herrnson (2012), Jacobson (2012), Campbell (1993), Kahn and Kenney (1999), or Kazee (1994) for congressional campaigns. Brewer and Maisel (2012) offers a comprehensive examination of state and local elections; it is highly recommended as additional reading beyond what we can cover in this book.

4. See, for example, Thurber and Nelson (1995; 2000; 2004), Johnson (2000; 2007), Dulio (2004), Medvic (2001), and Perlmutter (1999). More recent work includes Cain (2011), Panagopoulos and Weilhouwer (2008), Grossmann (2009), and Panagopoulos, Dulio, and Brewer (2011).

5. For 2008, see Pew Research Center Journalism Project, "Winning the Media Campaign: How the Press Reported the 2008 General Election," October 22, 2008, http://www.journalism.org/2008/10/22/winning-media-campaign; for 2012, see Pew Research Center Journalism Project, "Winning the Media Campaign 2012," November 2, 2012, http://www.journalism.org/2012/11/02/winning-media-campaign-2012.

6. Data accessed from the question search feature at Pew Research Center for the People and the Press, http://www.people-press.org/question-search. This question was from the Pew Internet & American Life Project Poll, October 2012, http://www.people-press.org/question-search/?qid=1824732&pid=51&ccid=50#top.

7. Data accessed from the question search feature at Pew Research Center for the People and the Press, http://www.people-press.org/question-search. This question was from the Pew Internet & American Life Project Poll, November 2012, http://www.people-press.org/question-search/?qid=1821103&pid=51&ccid=50#top.

8. Data accessed from the question search feature at Pew Research Center for the People and the Press, http://www.people-press.org/question-search. This question was from the Pew Research Center for the People & the Press Political Survey, October 2010, http://www.people-press.org/question-search/?qid=1772491&pid=51&ccid=50#top. There were no later data available for this question as there was with the presidential election data above.

9. There is some debate in political science about whether this figure, known as the voting eligible population (VEP), is the appropriate figure to use rather than the voting age population (VAP). While VAP counts every resident of the United States over 18 years of age—the legal age to vote—some argue that VEP is more accurate because it does not count noncitizens or those ineligible to vote because they are in prison, on parole, or an ex-convict (the rules on who can vote after being convicted of a crime vary by state). We are in the camp that believes VEP is the best starting point. See Michael McDonald's excellent work on this on his website, United States Elections Project (http://www.electproject.org).

10. See Michael McDonald's archive of voter turnout data, "Voter Turnout," http://elections.gmu.edu/voter_turnout.htm (accessed September 3, 2014).

11. Like many topics in political science, the research on this subject is too voluminous to mention fully. For a sampling of work, see Connelly and Field (1944), Downs (1957), Riker and Ordeshook (1968), Wolfinger and Rosenstone (1980), McDonald and Popkin (2001), Ansolabehere and Konisky (2006), Green and Shachar (2000), and Leighley and Nagel (2013).

12. US Census Bureau, "Voting and Registration in the Election of November 2012—Detailed Tables," Table 1: Reported Voting and Registration, by Sex and Single Year of Age: November 2012, http://www.census.gov/hhes/www/socdemo/voting/publications/p20/2012/tables.html).

13. US Census Bureau, "Voting and Registration in the Election of November 2012—Detailed Tables, Table 4a: Reported Voting and Registration of the Citizen-Age

Population, for States: November 2012," http://www.census.gov/hhes/www/socdemo/voting/publications/p20/2012/tables.html.

14. US Census Bureau, "Voting and Registration in the Election of November 2012—Detailed Tables, Table 10: Reasons for Not Voting, by Selected Characteristics: November 2012," http://www.census.gov/hhes/www/socdemo/voting/publications/p20/2012/tables.html.

15. Vote totals were calculated by the authors using data from the Michigan Secretary of State website, http://www.mich.gov/sos/0,4670,7-127-1633_8722---,00.html (accessed October 21, 2014).

16. These electoral rules are called "plurality" rules. In a two-person race, the winner gets a majority of votes, but in races with three or more candidates, the winner does not need a majority; they only need to receive more votes than their opponents. These rules apply in contests where voters are choosing only one candidate. Most contests in the United States fall under single-member districts, where one person is selected to be in government. There are, however, some jurisdictions that use multiple-member districts. The rules noted here do not apply in these instances.

17. Texas Secretary of State, "Early Voting—November 2, 2012," http://www.sos.state.tx.us/elections/earlyvoting/2012/nov2.shtml (accessed January 12, 2014).

18. California Secretary of State, *Statement of Vote: November 6, 2012, General Election*, http://www.sos.ca.gov/elections/sov/2012-general/sov-complete.pdf.

19. National Conference of State Legislatures, "Early and Absentee Voting," http://www.ncsl.org/research/elections-and-campaigns/absentee-and-early-voting.aspx (accessed January 11, 2014).

20. We should note here that presidential candidates do have the option of participating in a public funding system that would provide government funds to their campaigns, reducing the need to continually raise money. There is a partial public funding system for the presidential primaries where the federal government provides matching funds on a dollar-for-dollar basis for every contribution up to $250. To participate, a candidate must first qualify for the system by showing a basic level of support for his or her campaign (raising $5,000 in each of 20 different states) in addition to seeking the nomination of a political party. More importantly, the candidate must agree to set spending limits for the primary (in 2012, this limit was $45.6 million). This was one of the main goals of those who started the program in the early 1970s. The law's supporters thought that by limiting the amount candidates could spend, they would keep the cost of campaigning down. This has hardly been successful in the last several elections. In 2000, George W. Bush was the first major party candidate to eschew the matching funds system. Since then, no serious candidate for the presidency has participated in the public funding system for the primary process. There is also a public funding system for the general election where once a candidate receives the nomination of his or her party, he or she is provided what amounts to a grant from the federal government to use for the

general election campaign. In 2012 the amount a candidate would have had to work with was over $91 million. However, 2012 was also the year when, for the first time, neither major party candidate participated in this voluntary system during the general election. Why would they? Taken together, the 2012 spending limit for the primary and general elections was $136.8 million. Barack Obama raised over $700 million and Mitt Romney raised almost $450 million. If candidates can raise far more than the spending limits, they have no reason to participate in the system. For more on the public funding system, see Federal Election Commission, "Public Funding of Presidential Elections," August 1996 (updated April 2014), http://www.fec.gov/pages/brochures/pubfund.shtml.

21.   Campaign Finance Institute, "Senate Incumbents and Challengers, by Election Outcome," http://www.cfinst.org/federal/congress.aspx (accessed January 14, 2014).

22.   Campaign Finance Institute, "House Incumbents and Challengers, by Election Outcome," http://www.cfinst.org/ pdf/vital/VitalStats_t3.pdf (accessed January 14, 2014).

23.   The Center for Responsive Politics provides a number of election-related statistics about previous elections. See their "Election Stats" page at http://www.opensecrets .org/bigpicture/elec_stats.php?cycle=2012.

24.   The National Institute on Money in State Politics tracks campaign finance in all 50 states. Data on state-level spending in this section are taken from their website, http://www.followthemoney.org (accessed January 14, 2014).

25.   It is interesting to note that in state-level races, more money was raised in non-presidential years than in presidential years (data from the National Institute on Money in State Politics can be found at http://www.followthemoney.org/database/IndustryTotals .phtml?y=2012&f=0&l=0&abbr=0&s=0). As one would expect, however, at the federal level, presidential years see much more activity (data from the Center for Responsive Politics are at http://www.opensecrets.org/bigpicture).

26.   These limits are set by statute and enforced by the Federal Election Commission (see "Contributions Limits 2013–14," http://www.fec.gov/pages/brochures /contriblimits.shtml). The limits are per candidate per election, which means each entity can make the maximum contribution in both the primary and general elections. Since the enactment of the 2002 Bipartisan Campaign Reform Act, the individual limit is indexed to inflation, which means it can increase from one election cycle to the next.

27.   The National Conference of State Legislatures provides information on limits in all 50 states; see "Contribution Limits: An Overview," October 3, 2011, http://www .ncsl.org/research/elections-and-campaigns/campaign-contribution-limits-overview .aspx.

28.   These limits are new for 2014. The legislature passed and the governor signed a bill doubling the previous limits in late 2013. See Oosting (2013).

29. California Fair Political Practices Commission, "California Contribution Limits: Fast Facts," 2010, http://www.fppc.ca.gov/bulletin/Contriblimit201011.pdf.

30. The *Washington Post* created a useful feature that tracked ad spending during this election; see "Mad Money: TV Ads in the 2012 Presidential Campaign," http://www.washingtonpost.com/wp-srv/special/politics/track-presidential-campaign-ads-2012 (accessed January 12, 2014).

31. Pew Research Center, "Internet Use Over Time," Pew Research Internet Project, January 2014, http://www.pewinternet.org/data-trend/internet-use/internet-use-over-time.

32. Pew Research Center, "Social Media Use Over Time," Pew Research Internet Project, January 2014, http://www.pewinternet.org/data-trend/social-media/social-media-use-all-users.

33. See the Center for Responsive Politics report on party fund-raising, "Political Parties," http://www.opensecrets.org/parties/index.php?cmte=&cycle=2012 (accessed January 6, 2014).

34. See Dulio and Garrett (2007) for an examination of the differences across state parties in terms of strength.

35. See National Institute on Money in State Politics, "National Overview Map," http://www.followthemoney.org/database/nationalview.phtml?l=0&f=P&y=2012&abbr=0 (accessed January 11, 2014).

36. Exit polls are taken from CNN, "President: Full Results," December 10, 2012, http://www.cnn.com/election/2012/results/race/president. For scholarly evidence, see, for instance, Abramowitz (2010).

37. There are ways in which parties and their members choose candidates other than primaries. They may have a caucus or a party convention, for example. But direct primaries are the most familiar mechanism in modern American politics.

38. In addition, candidates in presidential nominating contests are not simply looking for votes. They are working to win delegates to their party's national nominating convention—typically held in late summer—where the nomination will formally be made. For more on this and presidential primaries in general, see Polsby et al. (2011), Norrander (2010), Sides et al. (2013), and Kamarck (2009).

39. The Tillman Act in 1907 prohibited monetary campaign contributions by corporations. The Smith-Connally Act (1943) and the Taft-Hartley Act (1947) extended this ban to contributions by unions.

40. See Center for Responsive Politics, "PAC Summary: Total Raised/Total to Candidates," http://www.opensecrets.org/pacs (accessed January 11, 2014).

41. See Center for Responsive Politics, "Outside Spending," http://www.opensecrets.org/outsidespending/fes_summ.php?cycle=2012 (accessed January 14, 2014).

## Chapter 2

1.  There are many ways to divide the elements of a campaign plan. We have divided the plan into ten sections. Others may have different divisions of tasks and divide the plan differently. The important point should not be the number of sections a plan has but the information contained therein.

2.  "Ted Kennedy: Why Do You Want to Be President?" YouTube video, posted by chrisjo33, October 10, 2008, http://www.youtube.com/watch?v=TDh2iKzBh4E.

3.  "Cafferty: Palin Should Scare the Hell Out of You," YouTube video, posted by heathr456, September 26, 2008, http://www.youtube.com/watch?v=D6XvedQbaQo.

## Chapter 3

1.  For example, see Southern California Association of Governments, *Profile of Riverside County*, May 2013, http://www.scag.ca.gov/Documents/RiversideCounty2.pdf.

2.  See Burton and Shea (2010) for other methods of estimating turnout.

3.  This is obviously for a two-person contest. Races where three or more candidates are running present a much more complex picture; see Burton and Shea (2010) for a discussion of these issues.

4.  See Burton and Shea (2010) for a discussion of ethics in conducting opposition research.

## Chapter 4

1.  For more on different kinds of crises in campaigns, see Garrett (2010).

2.  Several books outline these tactics and techniques more specifically than we do here. For more information on the specifics of campaign fund-raising, see, for instance, Burton and Shea (2010), Faucheux (2002), or Shaw (2014).

3.  These additional exercises are not tied to any specific case chapters. The scenarios presented could happen in any race around the nation. Many of them are based on actual events.

4.  Some of these exercises were taken from or are adjusted versions of those created by Alan Mann, former director of public opinion research for the Michigan House Republican Caucus. Our thanks to Mr. Mann for allowing us to use and revise some of them.

5.  The exercises in this section have been reprinted or draw heavily on exercises that appear in the curriculum guide prepared by the Center for Congressional and

Presidential Studies at American University, *Ethics in Campaign Politics: A Curriculum Study Guide for Universities*, 2002. We are grateful to the Center's director, James A. Thurber, for granting us permission to reprint these exercises, and to Carol Whitney, the original developer of the curriculum.

## Chapter 5

1. For details on this hiccup, see Arlette Saenz and Emily Friedman, "Rick Perry's Debate Lapse: 'Oops'—Can't Remember Department of Energy," ABC News, November 9, 2011, http://abcnews.go.com/blogs/politics/2011/11/rick-perrys-debate -lapse-oops-cant-remember-department-of-energy. For a video, see "Perry Stumbles at GOP Debate," YouTube video, posted by CBS News, November 9, 2011, http://www .youtube.com/watch?v=EZYQ9IYeOlU.

2. See "Overview of the Texas Economy," provided by the governor's office at http://governor.state.tx.us/files/ecodev/texas-economic-overview.pdf (accessed January 28, 2014).

3. World Bank, "GDP Ranking," http://data.worldbank.org/data-catalog/GDP -ranking-table (accessed January 22, 2014).

4. These data are taken from the Texas Politics Project at the University of Texas at Austin, "Tea Party Identification" (February 2010–February 2014)," http://texaspolitics .utexas.edu/archive/html/poll/features/tea_party_id/slide1.html (accessed September 15, 2014). Full question wording: "Suppose the Tea Party movement organized itself as a political party. When thinking about the next election for Congress, would you vote for the Republican candidate from your district, the Democratic candidate from your district, or the Tea Party candidate from your district?"

5. See Maxwell, Crain, and Santos (2014) for a detailed description of turnout in Texas and theories on why the relatively low turnout exists.

6. This was not always the case; in the past, impediments to voting such as the poll tax, the white primary, long residency requirements, and yearly registration existed in Texas.

7. United States Elections Project, "2012 General Election Turnout Rates," July 22, 2013, http://elections.gmu.edu/Turnout_2012G.html.

8. The lawsuit was brought by a number of parties, including the Mexican American Legislative Caucus; the district court opinion can be found at http://www.tlc.state .tx.us/redist/pdf/2011_0927_DOJ_issues.pdf (accessed January 26, 2014).

9. The decision can be found here: http://www.tlc.state.tx.us/redist/pdf /news_announcements/h309_690.pdf (accessed January 26, 2014).

10. These figures are taken from the district court decision noted above. After the 2012 elections, the legal battles did not stop. See the Texas Legislative Council's

redistricting resources, including a chronology of major events in the 2011 redistricting battle, at http://www.tlc.state.tx.us/redist/redist.html (accessed January 26, 2014). The legislature passed a new plan for the 2014 elections in mid-2013. However, there were no changes to the 144th in this new round of map drawing. The district court declared in September 2013 that this would be an interim plan for the 2014 elections. We note this here because it is possible that the district boundaries will change again.

## Chapter 6

1. See State of Michigan, "Michigan Economy: Agriculture," http://www.netstate .com/economy/mi_economy.htm (accessed February 19, 2014).

2. See US Census Bureau, "State and County Quick Facts: Michigan," http:// quickfacts.census.gov/qfd/states/26000.html (accessed February 16, 2014).

3. US Supreme Court cases involving "one person, one vote" decisions include *Wesberry v. Sanders* (1964), *Reynolds v. Sims* (1964), and *Baker v. Carr* (1962).

4. Michigan Secretary of State, "General Election Voter Registration/Turnout Statistics," http://www.michigan.gov/sos/0,4670,7-127-1633_8722-29616—,00.html (accessed February 19, 2014).

5. Michigan Secretary of State, Bureau of Elections, *Election Officials Manual, Chapter 2 Voter Registration,* http://www.michigan.gov/documents/sos/II_Voter _Registration_265983_7.pdf (accessed February 19, 2014).

6. This biographical information is drawn from Holly Hughes's biography page on her campaign website (http://hollyhughes.com/meet_holly.php).

7. This biographical information is drawn from an interview with Lamonte by the authors and from her campaign website (her 2014 website is http://collenelamonte .com) and state representative website (for 2014, http://091.housedems.com).

## Chapter 7

1. US Census Bureau, "State and County Quick Facts: Virginia," http://quick facts.census.gov/qfd/states/51000.html (accessed November 17, 2013).

2. US Census Bureau, "Virginia Quick Facts," http://quickfacts.census.gov/qfd /states/51000.html (accessed November 17, 2013).

3. Lydia Saad, "Not as Many U.S. States Lean Democratic in 2013," Gallup, January 29, 2014, http://www.gallup.com/poll/167030/not_states_lean_democratic_2013.aspx.

4. For district boundary description, see Commonwealth of Virginia, Division of Legislative Services, "District Boundary Descriptions," http://redistricting.dls.virginia .gov/2010/BoundaryDescriptions.aspx, accessed November 10, 2013.

5. US Census Bureau, "State and County QuickFacts: Newport News City, Virginia," http://quickfacts.census.gov/qfd/states/51/51700.html, accessed November 9, 2013.

6. David E. Yancey biographical information taken from Ballotpedia, "David Yancey," http://ballotpedia.org/David_Yancey; Virginia House of Delegates, "Delegate David E. Yancey," http://dela.state.va.us/dela/MemBios.nsf/a7b082ef6ed01eac85256c0d00515644/e3387958e627dae48525753500577406?OpenDocument&Click=85256823005F1997.f0a3d2c6f9f07af1852570bd00646e36/$Body/0.1A96; and the candidate's campaign website, http://davidyanceyfordelegate.com. All accessed November 9, 2013.

7. Robert Farinholt biographical information taken from Ballotpedia, "Robert Farinholt, Jr.," http://ballotpedia.org/Robert_Farinholt,_Jr.; Project Vote Smart, "Robert Farinholt Jr.'s Biography," http://votesmart.org/candidate/biography/144855/robert-farinholt-jr; WAVY-TV, "Robert C. Farinholt, Jr.," http://www.wavy.com/news/robert-c-farinholt-jr; and Vote VA, "Biographical Profile for Robert C. Farinholt, Jr.," http://vote-va.org/Intro.aspx?State=VA&Id=VAFARINHOLTROBERTCJR. All accessed November 16, 2013.

## Chapter 8

1. For more on this team of consultants, see Online Archive of California, "Inventory of the Whitaker & Baxter Campaigns, Inc. Records," http://www.oac.cdlib.org/findaid/ark:/13030/kt7p3036z9 (accessed September 8, 2014).

2. US Census Bureau, "State & County QuickFacts: California," http://quickfacts.census.gov/qfd/states/06000.html (accessed November 1, 2013).

3. For more on California's election administration in this area, see California Secretary of State, "Vote By Mail," http://www.sos.ca.gov/elections/elections_m.htm#perm (accessed November 1, 2013).

4. These calculations were made by the California Secretary of State; see "Historical Vote-By-Mail (Absentee) Ballot Use in California," http://www.sos.ca.gov/elections/hist_absentee.htm (accessed November 3, 2013).

5. National Institute on Money in State Politics, "California 2012, Party Committees," http://www.followthemoney.org/database/StateGlance/contributor_details.phtml?s=CA&y=2012&i=132 (accessed November 3, 2013).

6. See California Fair Political Practices Commission, "California Contribution Limits Fast Facts," http://fppc.ca.gov/bulletin/Contriblimit201011.pdf (accessed November 3, 2013).

7. Center for Responsive Politics, "2012 Presidential Race: Top States," http://www.opensecrets.org/pres12/index.php (accessed November 3, 2013).

8. See California Constitution, Article II, Section 8, available at http://ballot pedia.org/wiki/index.php/Article_II,_California_Constitution#Section_8 (accessed November 4, 2013).

9. The University of California Hastings Law Library's California Ballot Measures Database archives voter guides for all ballot propositions through the primary 2012 election at http://library.uchastings.edu/research/online-research/ballots.php.

10. For more information on the redistricting process, see the California Citizens Redistricting Commission website at http://wedrawthelines.ca.gov.

11. Registration data are taken from the California Secretary of State, "Voter Registration Statistics, 2012, 15-day Report of Registration," http://www.sos.ca.gov /elections/ror/ror-pages/15day-general-12/assembly1.pdf (accessed November 5, 2013).

12. Biographical information is drawn from Eric Linder's biography on his campaign website (http://ericlinder.com/erics_story) and from his official assemblyman website (http://arc.asm.ca.gov/member/AD60/?p=bio).

13. Information on Corona can be found, for example, at City Data, "Corona, California," http://www.city-data.com/city/Corona-California.html (accessed November 6, 2013).

14. Biographical information for Jose Luis Perez is drawn from his campaign's Facebook page, https://www.facebook.com/pages/Jose-Luis-Perez-for-California-60th -Assembly-District/316923418367197?sk=info (accessed November 7, 2013).

## Chapter 9

1. For more on Tip O'Neill, see O'Neill and Hymel (1995).

2. The full text of Clinton's speech can be found at http://clinton4.nara.gov /WH/New/other/sotu.html (accessed January 21, 2014).

# References

Abbey-Lambetz, Kate. 2013. "Janice Daniels, Michigan Mayor Who Was Recalled After Anti-Gay Slurs, Is Back." *Huffington Post*, August 14. http://www.huffingtonpost .com/2013/08/14/janice-daniels-troy-michigan-city-council_n_3757459.html.

Abramowitz, Alan I. 1983. "Partisan Redistricting and the 1983 Congressional Elections." *Journal of Politics* 45 (3): 767–770.

———. 2010. *The Disappearing Center: Engaged Citizens, Polarization, and American Democracy*. New Haven, CT: Yale University Press.

Abramowitz, Alan I., Brad Alexander, and Matthew Gunning. 2006. "Incumbency, Redistricting, and the Decline of Competition in U.S. House Elections." *Journal of Politics* 68 (1): 75–88.

Agranoff, Robert. 1972. *The New Style in Election Campaigns*. Boston: Holbrook Press.

Aldrich, John. 2011. *Why Parties? A Second Look*. Chicago: University of Chicago Press.

Alexander, Dave. 2012a. "Election 2012 Results: Democrat Collene Lamonte Shocks Holly Hughes in the 91st District." mlive.com, November 7. http://www.mlive .com/news/muskegon/index.ssf/2012/11/election_2012_results_democrat.html.

———. 2012b. "Muskegon County's 91st House District Has Been a Michigan Battle Ground for Years." mlive.com, October 5. http://www.mlive.com/news/muskegon /index.ssf/2012/10/muskegon_countys_91st_house_di.html.

Ansolabehere, Stephen, and David M. Konisky. 2006. "The Introduction of Voter Registration and Its Effect on Turnout." *Political Analysis* 14 (1): 83–100.

Batheja, Aman. 2012. "Impact of Late Legislators Is Felt in HD-144 Race." *Texas Tribune*, October 25. http://www.texastribune.org/2012/10/25 /deceased-lawmakers-playing-unique-role-hd-144-race.

Beaudry, Ann, and Bob Schaeffer. 1986. *Winning State and Local Elections*. New York: Free Press.

Bonneau, Chris, and Melinda G. Hall. 2009. *In Defense of Judicial Elections*. New York: Routledge.

Brewer, Mark D., and L. Sandy Maisel. 2012. *The Parties Respond: Changes in American Parties and Campaigns*. Boulder, CO: Westview Press.

Burton, Michael John, and Daniel M. Shea. 2010. *Campaign Craft: The Strategies, Tactics and Art of Political Campaign Management.* 4th ed. Santa Barbara, CA: Praeger.

Cain, Bruce. 1985. "Assessing the Partisan Effects of Redistricting." *American Political Science Review* 79 (2): 320–333.

Cain, Sean A. 2011. "An Elite Theory of Political Consulting and Its Implications for U.S. House Election Competition." *Political Behavior* 33 (3): 375–405.

Cameron, C., D. Epstein, and S. O'Halloran. 1996. "Do Majority-Minority Districts Maximize Substantive Black Representation in Congress?" *American Political Science Review* 9 (4): 794–812.

Campbell, James E. 1993. *The Presidential Pulse of Congressional Elections.* Lexington: University Press of Kentucky.

———. 2000. *American Campaign: U.S. Presidential Campaigns and the National Vote.* College Station, TX: Texas A&M University Press.

Casey, Chris. 1996. *The Hill on the Net: Congress Enters the Information Age.* Boston: AP Professional.

Chen, Jowei, and Jonathan Rodden. 2013. "Unintentional Gerrymandering: Political Geography and Electoral Bias in Legislatures." *Quarterly Journal of Political Science*, no. 8, 239–269.

Connelly, Gordon M., and Harry H. Field. 1944. "The Non-Voter—Who He Is, What He Thinks." *Public Opinion Quarterly* 8 (2): 175–187.

Cox, G. W., and J. N. Katz. 2002. *Elbridge Gerry's Salamander: The Electoral Consequences of the Reapportionment Revolution.* Cambridge: Cambridge University Press.

Delany, Colin. 2014. *How to Use the Internet to Win in 2014: A Comprehensive Guide to Online Politics for Campaigns and Advocates: Version 2.0.* Epolitics.com (Kindle).

Downs, Anthony. 1957. *An Economic Theory of Democracy.* New York: Harper and Row.

Dulio, David A. 2004. *For Better or Worse? How Professional Political Consultants Are Changing Elections in the United States.* Albany: State University of New York Press.

Dulio, David A., and R. Sam Garrett. 2007. "Organizational Strength and Campaign Professionalism in State Parties." In *State of the Parties: The Changing Role of Contemporary American Parties*, edited by John C. Green and Daniel J. Coffee, 199–216. Lanham, MD: Rowman and Littlefield.

Dye, Thomas. 2000. *Politics in States and Communities.* 10th ed. Upper Saddle River, NJ: Prentice Hall.

Farrell, David M. 1996. "Campaign Strategies and Tactics." In *Comparing Democracies: Elections and Voting in Global Perspective*, edited by Lawrence LeDuc, Richard G. Niemi, and Pippa Norris, 160–183. Thousand Oaks, CA: Sage Publications.

Faucheux, Ronald A. 2002. *Running for Office: The Strategies, Techniques, and Messages Modern Campaigns Need to Win Elections.* Lanham, MD: M. Evans and Company.

———. 2004. "Writing Your Campaign Plan: The Seven Components of Winning an Election." *Campaigns and Elections* 25 (3): 26.

Fenno, Richard F., Jr. 1978. *Home Style: House Members in Their Districts.* Boston: Little Brown.

Garrett, R. Sam. 2010. *Campaign Crises: Detours on the Road to Congress.* Boulder, CO: Lynne Rienner Publishers.

———. 2013. "Super PACs in Federal Elections: Overview and Issues for Congress." Congressional Research Report R42042, April 4.

Gerston, Larry N., and Terry Christensen. 2013. *California Politics and Government: A Practical Approach.* Stamford, CT: Cengage.

Goedert, Nicholas. 2012. "Not Gerrymandering, but Districting: More Evidence on How Democrats Won the Popular Vote but Lost the Congress." The Monkey Cage, November 15. http://themonkeycage.org/2012/11/15/not-gerrymandering-but -districting-more-evidence-on-how-democrats-won-the-popular-vote-but-lost-the -congress.

Gray, Virginia, Russell L. Hanson, and Thad Kousser, eds. 2013. *Politics in the American States: A Comparative Analysis.* 10th ed. Thousand Oaks, CA: Sage/CQ Press.

Green, Donald P., and Ron Shachar. 2000. "Habit Formation and Political Behaviour: Evidence of Consuetude in Voter Turnout." *British Journal of Political Science* 30 (4): 561–573.

Green, J. 2012. "Obama's CEO: Jim Messina Has a President to Sell." Bloomberg Businessweek, June 14. http://www.businessweek.com/articles/2012-06-14 /obamas-ceo-jim-messina-has-a-president-to-sell.

Grey, Lawrence. 2007. *How to Win a Local Election.* Lanham, MD: M. Evans and Company.

Griggs, D., and J. Katz. 2005. "The Impact of Majority-Minority Districts on Congressional Elections." Unpublished paper, California Institute of Technology.

Grossmann, Matt. 2009. "Going Pro? Political Campaign Consultants and the Professional Model." *Journal of Political Marketing* 8 (2): 81–104.

Haag, Stefan D., Gary A. Keith, and Rex C. Pebbles. 2003. *Texas Politics and Government: Ideas, Institutions, and Policies.* 3rd ed., Election Update. New York: Longman.

Haenschen, Katherine. 2012. "Burnt Orange Report's Guide to Texas's 2012 State House Races: Part I." Burnt Orange Report, May 3. http://www.burntorangereport.com /diary/12221/burnt-orange-reports-guide-to-texass-2012-state-house-races-part-i.

Herrnson, Paul S. 1988. *Party Campaigning in the 1980s.* Cambridge, MA: Harvard University Press.

———. 2004. *Congressional Elections: Campaigning at Home and in Washington.* 4th ed. Washington, DC: CQ Press.

———. 2012. *Congressional Elections: Campaigning at Home and in Washington.* 6th ed. Thousand Oaks, CA: Sage/CQ Press.

Herron, M., and A. Wiseman. 2008. "Gerrymanders and Theories of Law Making: A Study of Legislative Redistricting in Illinois." *Journal of Politics* 70 (1): 151–167.

Hershey, Marjorie Randon. 2014. *Party Politics in America.* 16th ed. Boston: Pearson.

Hill, K. A. 1995. "Does the Creation of Majority Black Districts Aid Republicans? An Analysis of the 1992 Congressional Elections in Eight Southern States." *Journal of Politics* 57 (2): 384–401.

Holbrook, Thomas. 1996. *Do Campaigns Matter?* Thousand Oaks, CA: Sage Publications.

Holley, Joe. 2012. "Legler Says No Mas." *Houston Chronicle*, March 7. http://blog.chron.com/texaspolitics/2012/03/legler-says-no-mas.

Houston Chronicle. 2012. "Perez for House District 144." *Houston Chronicle*, October 30. http://www.chron.com/opinion/editorials/article/Perez-for-House-District-144-3994652.php.

Issenberg, Sasha. 2012. *The Victory Lab: The Secret Science of Winning Campaigns*. New York: Crown Publishers.

Jackson, John S., III, and William Crotty. 2001. *The Politics of Presidential Selection*. 2nd ed. New York: Longman.

Jacobson, Gary C. 2012. *Politics of Congressional Elections*. Boston: Pearson.

Jennings, David. 2012. "Ted Cruz Fires Up the David Pineda Campaign." *Houston Chronicle*, October 24. http://blog.chron.com/bigjolly/2012/10/ted-cruz-fires-up-the-david-pineda-campaign/#8073101=0.

Johnson, Dennis W. 2000. "The Business of Political Consulting." In *Campaign Warriors: Political Consultants in Elections*, edited by James A. Thurber and Candice J. Nelson, 37–52. Washington, DC: Brookings Institution Press.

———. 2007. *No Place for Amateurs: Now Political Consultants Are Reshaping American Democracy*. London: Routledge Press.

Kahn, Kim Fridkin, and Patrick J. Kenney. 1999. "Do Negative Campaign Ads Mobilize or Suppress Turnout? Clarifying the Relationship Between Negativity and Participation." *American Political Science Review* 93 (4): 877–889.

Kamarck, Elaine C. 2009. *Primary Politics: Presidential Candidates and the Making of the Modern Nominating System*. Washington, DC: Brookings Institution Press.

Kayden, Xandra, and Eddie Mahe Jr. 1985. *The Party Goes On: The Persistence of the Two-Party System in the United States*. New York: Basic Books.

Kazee, Thomas A., ed. 1994. *Who Runs for Congress? Ambition, Context, and Candidate Emergence*. Washington, DC: CQ Press.

Keith, Gary A., Stefan Haag, Tucker L. Gibson Jr., and Clay Robison. 2012. *Texas Government and Politics*. 4th ed. Upper Saddle River, NJ: Pearson.

Klemanski, John S. 2013. "Trends in Michigan Supreme Court Elections 2000–2012." *Michigan Academician* 41 (3): 289–309.

Klemanski, John S., and David A. Dulio. 2006. *The Mechanics of State Legislative Campaigns*. Belmont, CA: Thomson Wadsworth.

Kolodny, Robin, and David A. Dulio. 2003. "Political Party Adaptation in US Congressional Campaigns." *Party Politics* 9 (6): 729–746.

Leighley, Jan E., and Jonathan Nagel. 2013. *Who Votes Now? Demographics, Issues, Inequality, and Turnout in the United States*. Princeton, NJ: Princeton University Press.

Lublin, D. 1997. *The Paradox of Representation: Racial Gerrymandering and Minority Interests in Congress*. Princeton, NJ: Princeton University Press.

Lyman, Rick. 2013. "Texas' Stringent Voter ID Law Makes a Dent at Polls." *New York Times*, November 6. http://www.nytimes.com/2013/11/07/us/politics/texas-stringent-voter-id-law-makes-a-dent-at-polls.html.

Maisel, L. Sandy. 2002. *Parties and Elections in America, Post-Election Update*. 3rd ed. Lanham, MD: Rowman and Littlefield Publishers.

Maxwell, William Earl, Ernest Crain, and Adolfo Santos. 2014. *Texas Politics Today: 2013–2014 Edition*. Stamford, CT: Cengage.

Mayer, William G., and Jonathan Bernstein, eds. 2012. *The Making of the Presidential Candidates 2012*. Lanham, MD: Rowman and Littlefield Publishers.

McCarty, N., K. T. Poole, and H. Rosenthal. 2009. "Does Gerrymandering Cause Polarization?" *American Journal of Political Science* 53 (3): 666–680.

McDonald, Michael P., and Samuel Popkin. 2001. "The Myth of the Vanishing Voter." *American Political Science Review* 95 (4): 963–974.

McKay, Amy. 2010. "The Effects of Interest Groups' Ideology on Their PAC and Lobbying Expenditures." *Business and Politics* 12 (2): Article 4.

Medvic, Stephen K. 2001. *Political Consultants in U.S. Congressional Elections*. Columbus: Ohio State University Press.

———. 2013. *Campaigns and Elections: Players and Processes*. 2nd ed. New York: Routledge.

Menefee-Libey, David. 2000. *The Triumph of Campaign-Centered Politics*. New York: Seven Bridges Press.

Miller, Arthur H., and Bruce E. Gronbeck. 1994. *Presidential Campaigns and American Self Images*. Boulder, CO: Westview Press.

Moncrief, Gary F., Peverill Squire, and Malcolm E. Jewell. 2000. *Who Runs for the Legislature?* Englewood Cliffs, NJ: Prentice Hall.

Murphy, Ryan. 2013. "Yancey to VA Congressional Delegation: 'Put Partisan Politics Aside' and Resolve Government Shutdown." *Daily Press*, October 11. http://www.dailypress.com/news/politics/shad-plank-blog/dp-yancey-to-va -congressional-delegation-put-partisan-politics-aside-and-resolve-government -shutdown-20131011,0,2008761.post.

Newport, Frank. 2014. "Congressional Re-Elect Measures Remains Near All-Time Low." Gallup, August 18. http://www.gallup.com/poll/174920/congressional -elect-measure-remains-near-time-low.aspx.

Norrander, Barbara. 2010. *The Imperfect Primary: Oddities, Biases, and Strengths of U.S. Presidential Nomination Politics*. New York: Routledge.

O'Neill, Tip, and Gary Hymel. 1995. *All Politics Is Local: And Other Rules of the Game*. Avon, MA: Adams Media Corporation.

Oosting, Jonathan. 2013. "Michigan Campaign Finance: 12 Things to Know about Controversial Bill to Double Donation Limits." mlive.com, December 13. http://www .mlive.com/politics/index.ssf/2013/12/michigan_campaign_finance_10_t.html.

Panagopoulos, Costas, David A. Dulio, and Sarah E. Brewer. 2011. "Lady Luck? Women Political Consultants in U.S. Congressional Campaigns." *Journal of Political Marketing* 10 (3): 251–274.

Panagopoulos, Costas, and Peter W. Weilhouwer. 2008. "The Ground War 2000–2004: Strategic Targeting in Grassroots Campaigns." *Presidential Studies Quarterly* 38 (2): 347–362.

Peaslee, Liliokanaio, and Nicholas J. Swartz. 2014. *Virginia Government: Institutions and Policy*. Thousand Oaks, CA: Sage/CQ Press.

Pelosi, Christine. 2012. *Campaign Boot Camp 2.0: Basic Training for Candidates, Staffers, Volunteers, and Nonprofits*. San Francisco: Berrett-Koehler Publishers.

Perlmutter, David. 1999. *The Manship School Guide to Political Communication*. Baton Rouge: Louisiana State University Press.

Peters, Jeremy W. 2012. "Limited Convention Broadcasts Shut Out Ann Romney." *New York Times*, August 22. http://www.nytimes.com/2012/08/23/us/politics/limited -convention-coverage-will-leave-ann-romney-off-air.html?pagewanted=all&_r=0.

Polsby, Nelson W., Aaron Wildavsky, Steven E. Shier, and David A. Hopkins. 2011. *Presidential Elections: Strategies and Structures of American Politics*. 13th ed. Lanham, MD: Rowman and Littlefield Publishers.

Pomper, Gerald M., ed. 2001. *The Election of 2000: Reports and Interpretations*. New York: Chatham House/Seven Bridges Press.

Powell, Larry, and Joseph Cowart. 2003. *Political Campaign Communication Inside and Out*. Boston: Allyn and Bacon.

Quist, Peter. 2012. "Super PAC Contributors Impact State Campaigns." National Institute on Money in State Politics, February 10. http://www.followthemoney.org /press/ReportView.phtml?r=479.

Ramsey, Ross. 2013. "UT/TT Poll: Abbott's Lead Over Davis in Single Digits." *Texas Tribune*, November 4. http://www.texastribune.org/2013/11/04 /uttt-poll-governor-race-abbott-leads-davis-6.

Ramsey, Ross, and Ryan Murphy. 2011. "The Texas Weekly Index: New Maps Heavily Favor GOP." *Texas Tribune*, September 21. http://www.texastribune. org/2011/09/21/texas-weekly-index-0921.

Riker, William, and Peter Ordeshook. 1968. "A Theory of the Calculus of Voting." *American Political Science Review* 62 (1): 25–42.

Romano, Lois. 2012. "Obama's Data Advantage." Politico, June 9. http://www.politico .com/news/stories/0612/77213.html.

Rutledge, Pamela. 2013. "Obama Successfully Harnessed Social Media." *National Psychologist* 22 (1): 12. http://nationalpsychologist.com/wp-content/uploads/2013/01 /NPJANFEB-2013.pdf.

Salmore, Barbara G., and Stephen A. Salmore. 1989. *Candidates, Parties, and Campaigns: Electoral Politics in America*. Washington, DC: CQ Press.

Schwartz, John. 2009. "Obama Seems to Be Open to a Broader Role for States." *New York Times*, January 30. http://www.nytimes.com/2009/01/30/us/politics/30federal .html?_r=1&.

Shaw, Catherine. 2014. *The Campaign Manager: Running and Winning Local Elections*. 5th ed. Boulder, CO: Westview Press.

Shea, Daniel M., Joanne Connor Green, and Christopher E. Smith. 2014. *Living Democracy*. 4th ed. New York: Pearson.

Sides, John, Daron Shaw, Matt Grossmann, and Keena Lipsitz. 2013. *Campaigns & Elections: Rules, Reality, Strategy, Choice*. New York: W.W. Norton.

Simpson, Dick. 2008. *Winning Elections: A Handbook in Modern Participatory Politics.* Boston: Pearson.

Skinner, Richard M., Seth E. Masket, and David A. Dulio. 2012. "527 Committees and the Party Network." *American Politics Research* 40 (1): 60–84.

Sorauf, Frank. 1994. *Inside Campaign Finance: Myths and Realities.* New Haven, CT: Yale University Press.

Thurber, James A. 2001. *The Battle for Congress: Consultants, Candidates, and Voters.* Washington, DC: Brookings Institution Press.

Thurber, James A., and Candice J. Nelson, eds. 1995. *Campaigns and Elections, American Style.* Boulder, CO: Westview Press.

———. 2000. *Campaign Warriors: Political Consultants in Elections.* Washington, DC: Brookings Institution Press.

———. 2004. *Campaigns and Elections, American Style.* 2nd ed. Boulder, CO: Westview Press.

Ting, Yuan, Stephen Stambough, and Shelly Arsenault. 2011. *California Government in National Perspective.* Dubuque, IA: Kendall Hunt Publishing.

Towner, Terri L. 2013. "All Political Participation Is Socially Networked? New Media in the 2012 Elections." *Social Science Computer Review* 31 (5): 527–541.

Towner, Terri L., and David A. Dulio. 2011. "An Experiment of Campaign Effects during the YouTube Election." *New Media & Society* 13 (4): 626–644.

Trende, Sean. 2013. "How Mich. Rebuts Redistricting/Polarization Claims." *RealClearPolitics,* October 15. http://www.realclearpolitics.com/articles/2013/10/15/how_mich_rebuts_redistrictingpolarization_claims_120323.html.

Troy, Gil. 1991. *See How They Ran: The Changing Role of the Presidential Candidate.* New York: Free Press.

Vavreck, Lynn. 2009. *The Message Matters: The Economy and Presidential Campaigns.* Princeton, NJ: Princeton University Press.

Wang, Sam. 2013. "The Great Gerrymander of 2012." *New York Times,* February 3: 1L.

Wattenberg, Martin P. 1992. *The Rise of Candidate-Centered Politics: Presidential Elections of the 1980s.* Cambridge, MA: Harvard University Press.

Wayne, Stephen J. 2001. *The Road to the White House 2000: The Politics of Presidential Elections, The Post Election Edition.* Bedford, MA: St. Martin's Press.

———. 2012. *The Road to the White House 2012.* Boston: Wadsworth Cengage Learning.

Wolfinger, Raymond E., and Stephen J. Rosenstone. 1980. *Who Votes?* New Haven, CT: Yale University Press.

# INDEX

Abramowitz, Alan I., 5
Absentee ballots, 13, 89, 101, 113, 132–133, 135, 146, 147
Affordable Care Act (2010), 4–5, 10, 59, 115, 148
Agranoff, Robert, 6, 28
Alexander, Brad, 5
Amash, Justin, 24
American Community Survey, 51
Americans for Tax Reform, Taxpayer Protection Pledge, 137
Anti-incumbency, 143

Bachmann, Michele, 23
Ballot initiatives, 133–134, 146
Ballot roll-off, 12–13, 144
Ballotpedia, 139
Base party vote, 55, 57–59, 62
Baxter, Leone, 131
Beaudry, Ann, 35
Biden, Joe, 23
Brown, Scott, 14
Budgets, 40–41, 74–79
Burton, Michael John, 7
Bush, George H. W., 97
Bush, George W., 97

Cafferty, Jack, 44
Cain, Herman, 23
Calendars. *See* Campaign calendars

California: campaign finance, 17; Citizens Redistricting Commission, 134, 146; early voter turnout, 13; Inland Empire, 136; primary system, xiii, 133, 134, 135, 146; Secretary of State, 132, 139; state's political context, 11, 12, 131–135, 146
California Assembly District 60, 131–140; base party vote, 57–58; campaign plan, web resources, 138–140; demographic analysis, 51; district characteristics, 135–137; Eric Linder, 137; Jose Luis Perez, 138; precincts in, 55; state's political context, 131–135
Calley, Brian, 24
Camp, Dave, 24
*Campaign Boot Camp 2.0* (Pelosi), 6
Campaign calendars, 45, 81, 90–92
Campaign communication, 17–20, 42–44
*Campaign Craft* (Burton and Shea), 7
Campaign ethics, 48–49, 94–95, 150–151
Campaign finance, 14–17, 143–144
Campaign Finance Institute, 14
*The Campaign Manager* (Shaw), 6
Campaign message, 38–40, 72–73
Campaign plans, 31–46; budgets and fund-raising, 40–41;

communication plans, 42–44;
creating of, 33–35; district analysis,
35–40; GOTV plans, 44–45;
in national context, 147–149;
organizing of, 32–33; volunteers,
41–42

Campaign simulation, 47–95; budgets
and fund-raising, 74–79; campaign
calendar, 81, 90–92; campaign
message, 72–73; crisis management
scenarios, 92–94; district and
demographic analysis, 49–52;
earned media, 87–89; electoral
research, 53–65; ethical dilemmas,
48–49, 94–95; GOTV plans,
89–90; opposition and candidate
research, 65–69; paid media,
82–87; volunteers, 80–82

Campaign themes, 40

Campaigns Inc., 131

Candidate, as source of funds, 74

Candidate-centered campaigns, 21

Carter, Jimmy, 97

Center for Responsive Politics, 16, 26, 27

Chen, Jowei, 5

*Citizens United v. Federal Election
    Commission*, xiii, 27, 113

Clinton, Bill, 142

Clinton, Hillary, 23

Communication plans, 17–20, 42–44

Community profile, 50–51

Cooley, Ken, 16

Core teams, 32–33

Couric, Katie, 44

Cox, Mike, 24

Crisis management, 92–94, 149–150

Cruz, Ted, 97, 100, 105

Cuccinelli, Ken, 124

Daniels, Janice, 37–38

Data mining, 84

Davis, Wendy, 97

Dean, Howard, 18

Delany, Colin, 6

Democratic Congressional Campaign
    Committee (DCCC), 20

Democratic National Committee
    (DNC), 20

Democratic Senatorial Campaign
    Committee (DSCC), 20

Demographic analysis, 51–52

DeVos, Dick, 24

Direct mail, 17, 26, 43, 76, 83–84

District analysis, 35–40, 49–52, 147–148.
    *See also specific districts*

Dodd, Chris, 23

Down-ballot races: campaign staffing
    in, 32; candidates for, 91;
    communications in, 42; GOTV
    efforts in, 44; vs. national and
    statewide campaigns, 7–29, 144–145;
    paid media in, 83, 85; use of
    technology in, 54, 76; volunteers
    in, 41; voter engagement in, 42

Early in-person voting, 13–14, 44, 101,
    146, 147

Earned media, 9, 43–44, 87–89

Economic analysis, 50–51

Edwards, John, 23

Elected officials, number of, 2

Elections: of 2000, 9; of 2004, 12; of
    2006, 12; of 2008, 8, 12, 14, 23,
    40, 104, 123; of 2010, 12; of 2012,
    5, 9, 10–15, 17, 21, 23, 26, 27,
    40, 97, 104, 110, 111, 123, 148;
    of 2013, 12. *See also specific house
    districts*

Electoral research, 53–65

Esch, Marvin, 111

Exercises: budgets and fund-raising,
    79; campaign calendars, 91;
    campaign message, 73; district and
    demographic analysis, 52; earned
    media, 88–89; electoral research,
    65; GOTV efforts, 90; opposition
    and candidate research, 69; paid
    media, 86–87; volunteers, 82

Facebook, xii, 18, 19, 37–38, 43, 76–77
Family and friends, 74, 80
Farinholt, Robert, 127
Farrell, David M., 28
Federal Election Campaign Act (1974 Amendments), 25
Federal Election Commission, 27
Fenno, Richard, 15
First Amendment, xiii, 27
501(c) organizations, 26–27
Ford, Gerald, 97, 110
Free media. *See* Earned media
Fund-raising, 41, 74–79

Gallup polls, 124, 143
Geographic analysis, 50
Gerrymandering, 5
Get-out-the-vote (GOTV), 28, 44–45, 89–90
Giuliani, Rudy, 23
Goedert, Nicholas, 5
Gravel, Mike, 23
Grey, Lawrence, 6
Gubernatorial campaigns, 9–10, 12, 54
Gunning, Matthew, 5

Henry, Patrick, 121
Hoekstra, Peter, 111
Horse race, use of term, 9
*How to Win a Local Election* (Grey), 6
Huckabee, Mike, 23
Hughes, Chris, 18
Hughes, Holly, 3, 115–116, 117
Huizenga, Bill, 111
Hunter, Duncan, 23
Huntsman, Jon, 23

Independent cities, 122
Instagram, 18, 19
Internet, 18–19. *See also* Social media
Issenberg, Sasha, 6
Issue activists, 81

Jefferson, Thomas, 121
Johnson, Lyndon B., 97

Keith, Gary A., 102
Kennedy, Edward, 38, 40
Keyes, Alan, 23
King, Angus, 15
Kucinich, Dennis, 23

Lamonte, Collene, 2–4, 116, 117
Land, Terri Lynn, 24
Lawn signs, 83
Legler, Ken, 104
Levin, Carl, 24
Lincoln, Abraham, 1, 40
Linder, Eric, 137
LinkedIn, 18
Literature drops, 83

Majority parties, 5
Margo, Don, 15
McAuliffe, Terry, 124
McCain, John, 18, 23, 40, 104
McCarthy, Kevin, 131
McDonald, Michael, 12
McDonnell, Bob, 124
*The Mechanics of State Legislative Campaigns* (Klemanski and Dulio), xii
Media attention, 8–10, 43–44, 82–89
Michigan: campaign finance, 16–17; data for district analysis, 58; Secretary of State, 113, 118, 119; state's political context, 11, 12, 110–113, 147; term limits, 3; voter turnout, 112
Michigan Education Association (MEA), 111
Michigan House District 40, 13
Michigan House District 91, 3, 5, 109–119; campaign plan, web resources, 117–119; Collene Lamonte, 116; demographic analysis, 51–52; district characteristics, 113–115; Holly Hughes, 115–116; Nick Sundquist, 116–117; state's political context, 110–113
Microtargeting, 17

Miller, Candice, 24
Moody, Joe, 15
Motor voter registration reforms, 64, 113
Multilingual voting materials, 102
*Muskegon Chronicle*, 115, 118
MyBarackObama.com, 18

Name identification, 83
National Institute on Money in State
    Politics, 16, 28, 108, 129
National nominating conventions, 9
National Republican Campaign
    Committee (NRCC), 20
National Republican Senatorial
    Committee (NRSC), 20
National Voter Registration Act (1993),
    113
Negative campaigning, 37, 73
Nixon, Richard, 131
No-excuse absentee voting, 113, 132–
    133, 146, 147
Norquist, Grover, 137

Obama, Barack, xii; campaign finance,
    14, 17; election of 2008, 23,
    40, 104, 123; election of 2012,
    21, 23, 40, 97, 104, 110, 111,
    123; leveraging of technology in
    campaigns, 18, 54, 77; progressive
    federalism of, 4, 142
Obamacare. *See* Affordable Care Act
Oder, Glenn, 127
O'Neill, Tip, 141
Opposition research, 36–37, 65–69,
    72–73
Organization of Petroleum Exporting
    Countries (OPEC), 98

Paid media, 82–87
Palin, Sarah, 44
Paul, Ron, 23, 123
Pelosi, Christine, 6
Pelosi, Nancy, 131
Perez, Jose Luis, 138

Perez, Mary Ann, 104–105
Perry, Rick, 23, 97, 104
Personal solicitations, 75–76
Peters, Gary, 24
Pew Research Center, 10–11, 18–19
Pineda, David, 105–106
Pinterest, 18
Political action committees (PACs),
    16–17, 25–27, 75
Political parties, 20–25, 75, 80–81,
    148–149
Precincts, 55. *See also* Electoral research
Presidential campaigns, 8–9, 10–11,
    14–15, 18, 53–54, 144. *See also*
    *specific presidential candidates*
*Press Enterprise*, 139
Primaries, 22–23, 133, 134, 135, 146
Project Vote Smart, 129
Pursell, Carl, 111

Ravel, Ann, 131
Reagan, Ronald, 111, 131, 142
Reagan Democrats, 111
Redistricting, 5, 143
Republican National Committee (RNC),
    20
Reynolds, Ron, 16
Richardson, Bill, 23
Robocalls, 18
Rodden, Jonathan, 5
Rogers, Mike, 24
Romney, Ann, 9
Romney, George, 110
Romney, Mitt, 110; campaign finance,
    14, 17; election of 2008, 23;
    election of 2012, 21, 23, 104, 111,
    123, 148
Romney, Scott, 24

Salience, 10–11, 43–44
Santorum, Rick, 23
Schaeffer, Bob, 35
Schuette, Bill, 24
Serrano, Jose E., 15

Shaw, Catherine, 6
Shea, Dan, 1, 7
Simpson, Dick, 6
Simulations. *See* Campaign simulation
Snyder, Rick, 3
Social media, xii, 18; GOTV efforts,
    89; leveraging of technology in
    campaigns, 18–20, 43, 54, 145;
    liability of, 37–38; online fund-
    raising, 76–77; use by American
    adults (2013), 18; video messages,
    85–86; volunteer mobilization, 82
*SpeechNow v. Federal Election
    Commission,* 27
State house campaigns, national
    context, 141–152; campaign ethics,
    150–151; and campaign plans,
    147–149; comparisons with state/
    national elections, 142–145; crisis
    management, 149–150; state
    variations, 145–147
State house campaigns, overview,
    1–30; campaign finance, 14–17;
    communications, 17–20; vs. down-
    ballot races, 7–29; electioneering
    principles, 28–29; literature review,
    6–7; media attention, 8–10; outside
    influences, 25–28; role of parties,
    20–25; salience, 10–11; voter
    turnout, 11–14
State legislative campaigns, 15–16,
    20–21, 24–25, 28, 41
Stauss, Joe, 15
Students, 81
Sundquist, Nick, 116–117
Super PACs, 22, 27–28
SWOT analysis, 38–39, 68–69, 72

Tateishi, Peter, 16
Tea Party, 100–101
Telephone calling programs, 18
Television advertising, 17, 19, 26, 43,
    84–86
Term limits, 24–25, 112, 122, 134, 146

Texas: data for district analysis, 58,
    106–107; early voter turnout,
    13–14; gross state product (GSP),
    99; state's political context, 11, 12,
    98–102, 147; Texan Creed, 101;
    voter turnout, 101
Texas House District 144, 5, 97–108;
    campaign plan, web resources,
    106–108; David Pineda, 105–106;
    district characteristics, 103–104;
    Mary Ann Perez, 104–105; state's
    political context, 98–102
Texas Legislative Council, 51, 58
Third-party candidates, 117
Thompson, Fred, 23
Ticketed events, 76
Top-two primaries, 22–23, 133, 134,
    135, 146
Trende, Sean, 5
Tumblr, 19
Twitter, xii, 18, 19, 43, 76–77

United Auto Workers (UAW), 111
United Way of America, 148
US Census Bureau, 12, 51, 99, 123
US House campaigns, 9–10, 11, 14–15,
    27–28
US Justice Department, 102
US Senate campaigns, 9–10, 11, 14–15,
    24, 27
US Supreme Court, 27, 103

Valentine, Mary, 3, 115
*The Victory Lab* (Issenberg), 6
Video messages, 84–85
Virginia: data for district analysis, 58;
    gubernatorial elections in, 12;
    State Board of Elections, 129;
    state's political context, 11, 12,
    122–124, 146
Virginia House of Delegates District
    94, 5, 121–130; campaign plan,
    web resources, 128–129; David
    E. Yancey, 126–127; demographic

analysis, 51; district characteristics, 124–126; precincts in, 55; Robert Farinholt, 127; state's political context, 122–124

Virginia Public Access Project, 128–129

Volunteers, 41–42, 80–82

Vote VA, 129

Vote-by-mail states, xiii

Voter identification laws, xiii, 102, 124

Voter mobilization. *See* Get-out-the-vote (GOTV)

Voter statistics, 54–65

Voter turnout, 11–14

Voting by mail, 13

Voting Rights Act (1965), 102

Wang, Sam, 5

Warren, Elizabeth, 14

Washington, George, 121

West, Allen, 15

Whitaker, Clem, 131

White, Bill, 104

*Winning Elections* (Simpson), 6

XIT (cattle ranch), 98

Yancey, David E., 126–127, 142

YouTube, 19, 75–76

# ABOUT THE AUTHORS

**John S. Klemanski** is a professor of political science at Oakland University, located in Rochester, Michigan. He has served as a campaign consultant for state legislative and judicial campaigns in Michigan since 1994 and was campaign manager for a state house race in Michigan. He is the author or coauthor of over thirty books, book chapters, and journal articles, mostly on campaigns, elections, and urban development politics and policy. His books include *The Urban Politics Dictionary*, *Power and City Governance*, *The Mechanics of State Legislative Campaigns*, and *Diversity in Contemporary American Politics and Government*.

**David A. Dulio** is a professor and chair of political science at Oakland University. He has published eight books, including *Cases in Congressional Campaigns: Riding the Wave*; *Vital Signs: Perspectives on the Health of American Campaigning*; and *For Better or Worse? How Professional Political Consultants are Changing Elections in the United States*. Previously he was an American Political Science Congressional Fellow on Capitol Hill, where he worked in the US House of Representatives Republican Conference for former US Representative J. C. Watts Jr. (R-OK).

**Michael Switalski** has served as a member of the Michigan State House and State Senate and as a city council member and a county commissioner. He currently is an elected treasurer for the city of Roseville, Michigan. He has run for office at all levels, including local, state, and federal offices. He has been a candidate in a total of twenty elections over the past twenty-four years and served twelve years in the Michigan legislature.